HOW TO MAKE AWESOME COMICS

WITH

HELLO!

OOK!

PROFESSOR PANELS **AND** **ART MONKEY**

BY NEILL CAMERON

David Fickling Books · the PHOENIX

SCHOLASTIC

Text copyright © 2017 and illustrations copyright © 2014 by Neill Cameron

All rights reserved. Published by Scholastic Inc., *Publishers since 1920*, by arrangement with David Fickling Books, Oxford, England. SCHOLASTIC and associated logos are trademarks and/or registered trademarks of Scholastic Inc. DAVID FICKLING BOOKS, THE PHOENIX, and associated logos are trademarks and/or registered trademarks of David Fickling Books.

First published in the United Kingdom in 2014
by David Fickling Books, 31 Beaumont Street, Oxford OX1 2NP.
www.davidficklingbooks.com

Library of Congress Cataloging-in-Publication Data available

ISBN 978-1-338-13273-1

10 9 8 7 6   20 21 22 23 24

Printed in China 38
First edition, May 2017

CONTENTS

CHAPTER 1

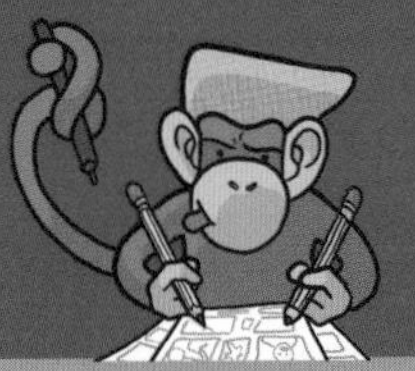

CHAPTER 2

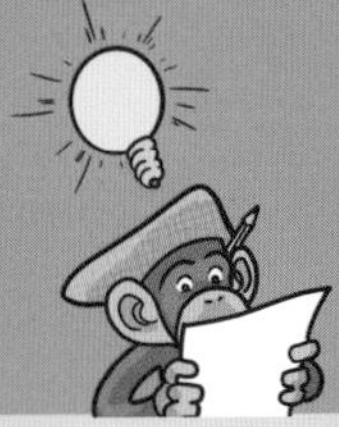

CHAPTER 3

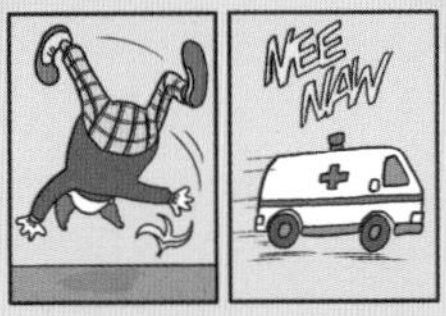

NEE NAW

CHAPTER 4

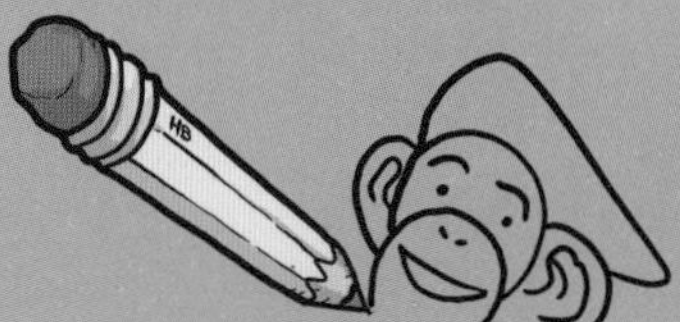

HB

CHAPTER 5

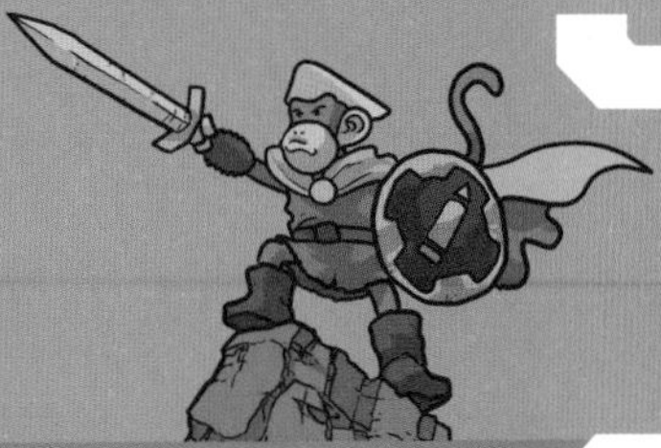

CHAPTER 6

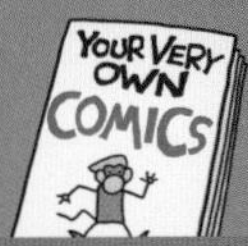

YOUR VERY OWN COMICS

I'M *PROFESSOR PANELS* – EMINENT AND WORLD-FAMOUS EXPERT ON ALL THINGS COMICS!

IN THIS BOOK I'M GOING TO TEACH YOU EVERYTHING YOU NEED TO KNOW TO CREATE YOUR VERY OWN *AWESOME COMICS!*

ALL YOU NEED IS:

1

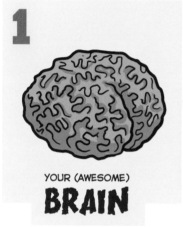

YOUR (AWESOME)
BRAIN

NOTE: DO NOT REMOVE FROM HEAD.

2

A
PENCIL

(OR PEN)

(WHATEVER, REALLY)

3

SOME
BANANAS

FOR SUSTENANCE!

(OPTIONAL)

...AND THAT'S IT. YOU'RE READY TO GO!

BY THE TIME WE GET TO THE END OF THIS BOOK, YOU WILL BE AN *EXPERT IN AWESOMOLOGY* AND A *COMICS-CREATING MASTER!*

DON'T BELIEVE ME? THERE'S ONLY ONE WAY TO FIND OUT...

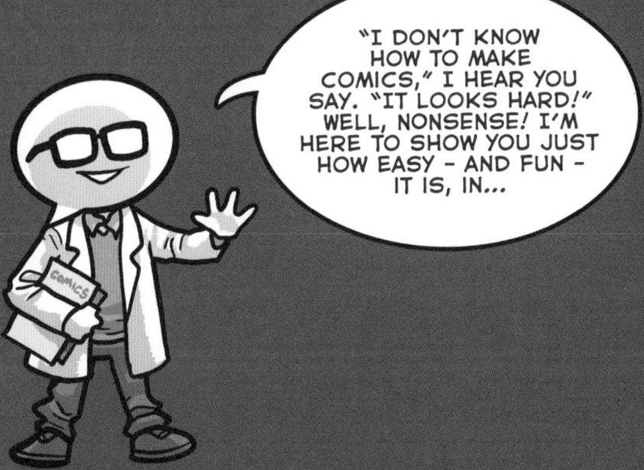
"I DON'T KNOW HOW TO MAKE COMICS," I HEAR YOU SAY. "IT LOOKS HARD!" WELL, NONSENSE! I'M HERE TO SHOW YOU JUST HOW EASY - AND FUN - IT IS, IN...
COMICS

CHAPTER 1

ANYONE CAN MAKE (AWESOME) COMICS

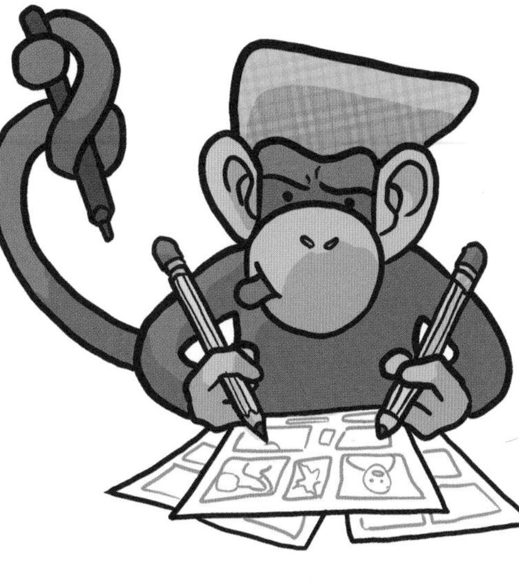

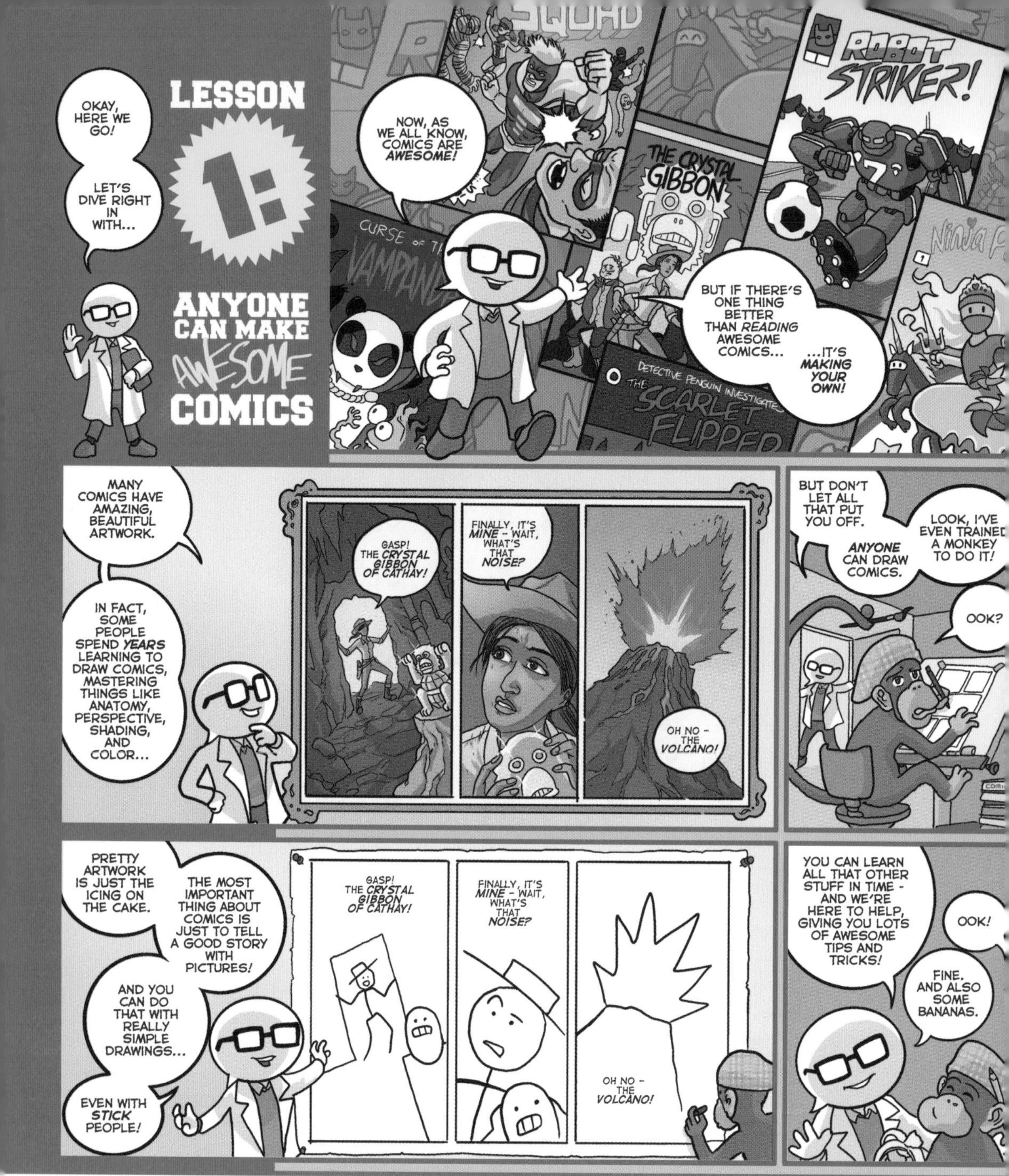

OKAY, HERE WE GO!
LET'S DIVE RIGHT IN WITH...
LESSON 1:
ANYONE CAN MAKE AWESOME COMICS
NOW, AS WE ALL KNOW, COMICS ARE *AWESOME!*
ROBOT STRIKER!
THE CRYSTAL GIBBON
CURSE OF THE VAMPANDA
BUT IF THERE'S ONE THING BETTER THAN *READING* AWESOME COMICS...
...IT'S *MAKING YOUR OWN!*
DETECTIVE PENGUIN INVESTIGATES THE SCARLET FLIPPER
MANY COMICS HAVE AMAZING, BEAUTIFUL ARTWORK.
IN FACT, SOME PEOPLE SPEND *YEARS* LEARNING TO DRAW COMICS, MASTERING THINGS LIKE ANATOMY, PERSPECTIVE, SHADING, AND COLOR...
GASP! THE *CRYSTAL GIBBON OF CATHAY!*
FINALLY, IT'S *MINE* - WAIT, WHAT'S THAT *NOISE?*
OH NO - THE *VOLCANO!*
BUT DON'T LET ALL THAT PUT YOU OFF.
ANYONE CAN DRAW COMICS.
LOOK, I'VE EVEN TRAINED A MONKEY TO DO IT!
OOK?
PRETTY ARTWORK IS JUST THE ICING ON THE CAKE.
THE MOST IMPORTANT THING ABOUT COMICS IS JUST TO TELL A GOOD STORY WITH PICTURES!
AND YOU CAN DO THAT WITH REALLY SIMPLE DRAWINGS...
EVEN WITH *STICK* PEOPLE!
GASP! THE *CRYSTAL GIBBON OF CATHAY!*
FINALLY, IT'S *MINE* - WAIT, WHAT'S THAT *NOISE?*
OH NO - THE *VOLCANO!*
YOU CAN LEARN ALL THAT OTHER STUFF IN TIME - AND WE'RE HERE TO HELP, GIVING YOU LOTS OF AWESOME TIPS AND TRICKS!
OOK!
FINE. AND ALSO SOME BANANAS.

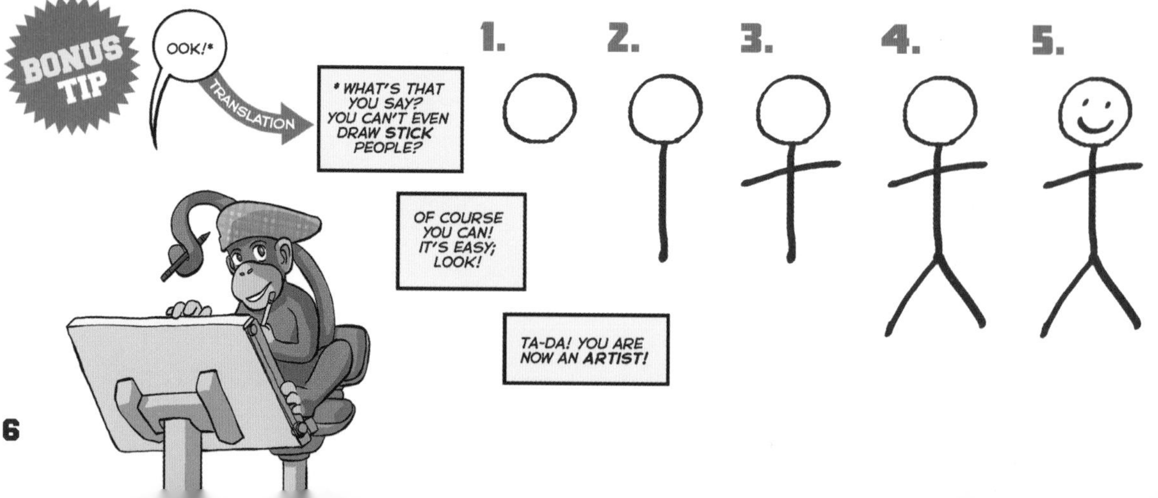

BONUS TIP
OOK!*
TRANSLATION
* WHAT'S THAT YOU SAY? YOU CAN'T EVEN DRAW **STICK** PEOPLE?
OF COURSE YOU CAN! IT'S EASY; LOOK!
1.
2.
3.
4.
5.
TA-DA! YOU ARE NOW AN **ARTIST!**

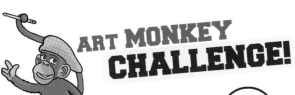

ART MONKEY CHALLENGE!

OOK!*

* OKAY, GUYS, IT'S YOUR TURN!

HERE'S A SIMPLE LITTLE COMIC STRIP STARRING TWO STICK PEOPLE.

BUT THE LAST PANEL'S BLANK - WHAT WILL HAPPEN? IT'S UP TO ***YOU!***

WELL, WELL, WELL! IT'S THE FAMOUS CAT BURGLAR, "FINGERS" JOHNSON!
OH NO, THE COPS!
SWAG
YOU'RE FINISHED, JOHNSON!
WAIT! I HAVE A SECRET! YOU SEE, I'M REALLY...
SWAG

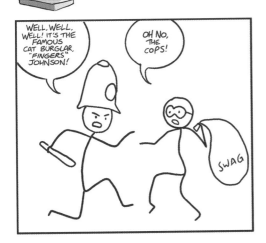

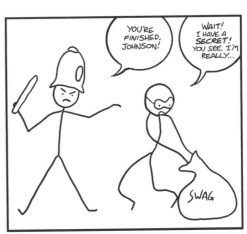

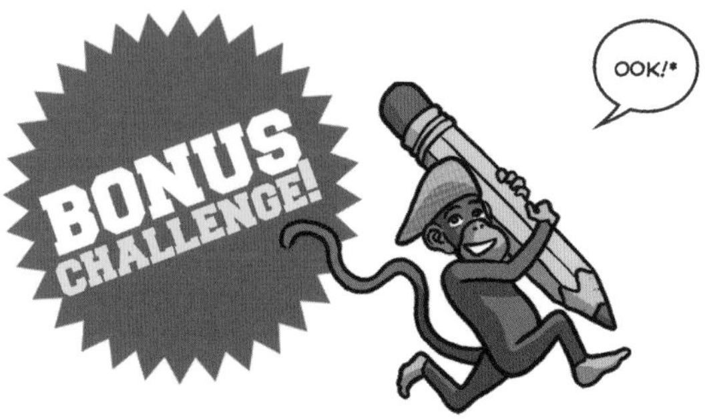
BONUS CHALLENGE!
OOK!*

* THAT WAS EASY, RIGHT? WHO'S READY FOR SOME MORE?

PSSST! YOU CAN TRY DRAWING IN SOME DIFFERENT STYLES, OR JUST KEEP USING STICK PEOPLE FOR NOW – IT'S UP TO *YOU!*

LEVEL 1

NICE AND EASY TO GET YOU STARTED! WE'VE LEFT THE LAST PANEL BLANK. WHAT HAPPENS NEXT? IT'S UP TO YOU!

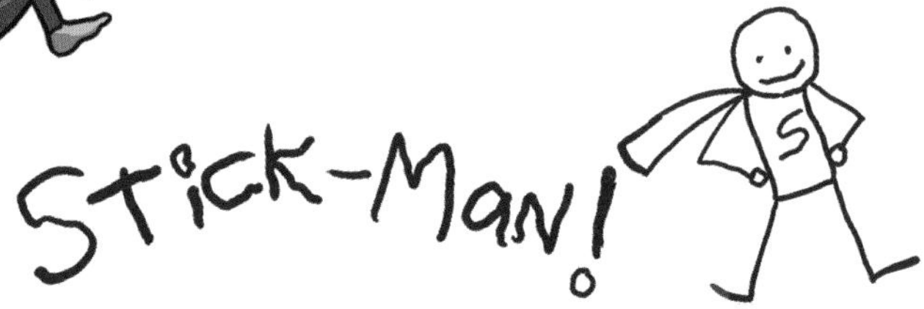
Stick-Man!

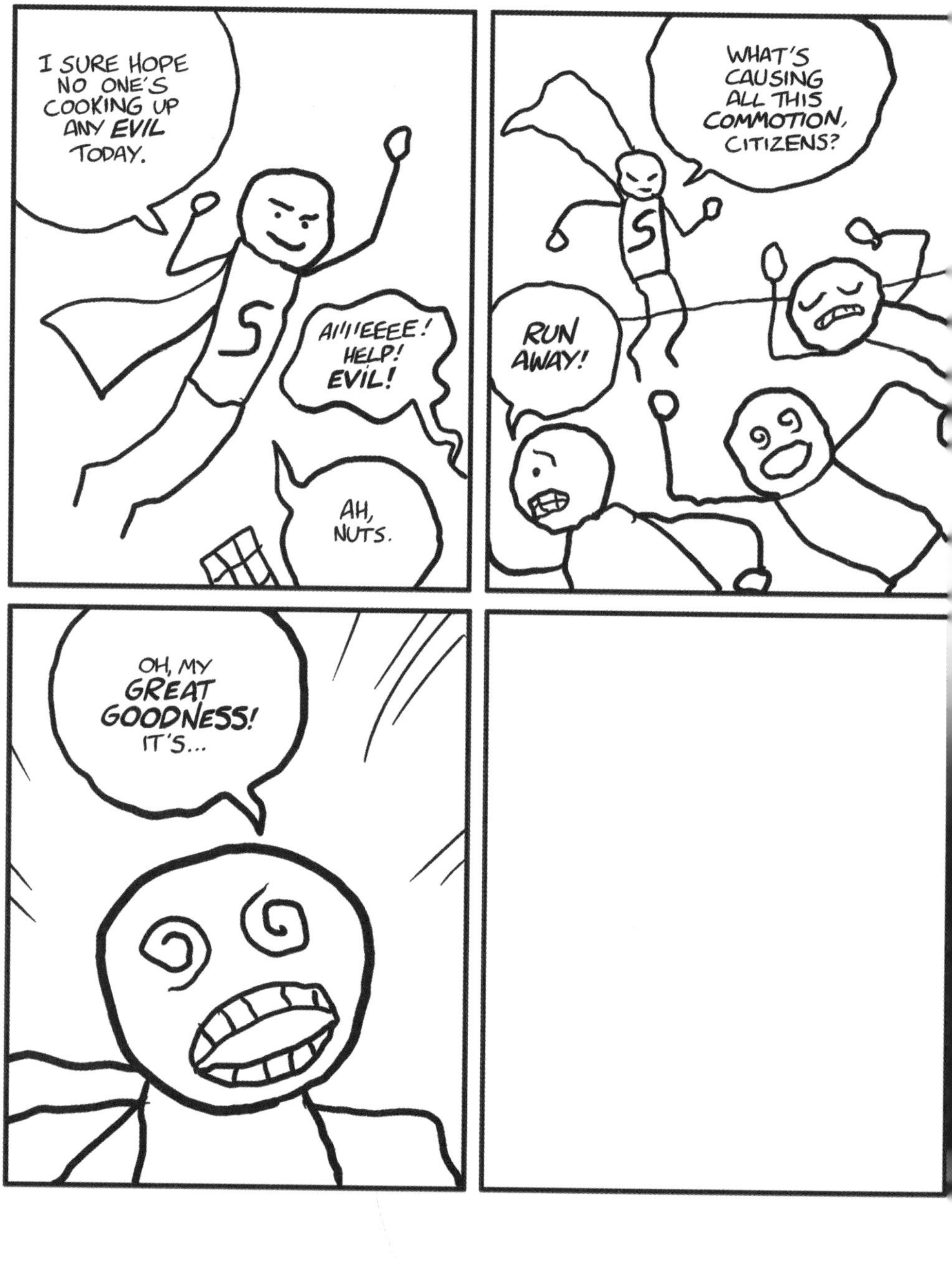
I SURE HOPE NO ONE'S COOKING UP ANY EVIL TODAY.
AIIIEEEE! HELP! EVIL!
AH, NUTS.
WHAT'S CAUSING ALL THIS COMMOTION, CITIZENS?
RUN AWAY!
OH, MY GREAT GOODNESS! IT'S...

LEVEL 2

NOW A BIT HARDER. THIS TIME WE'VE JUST GIVEN YOU THE FIRST TWO PANELS!

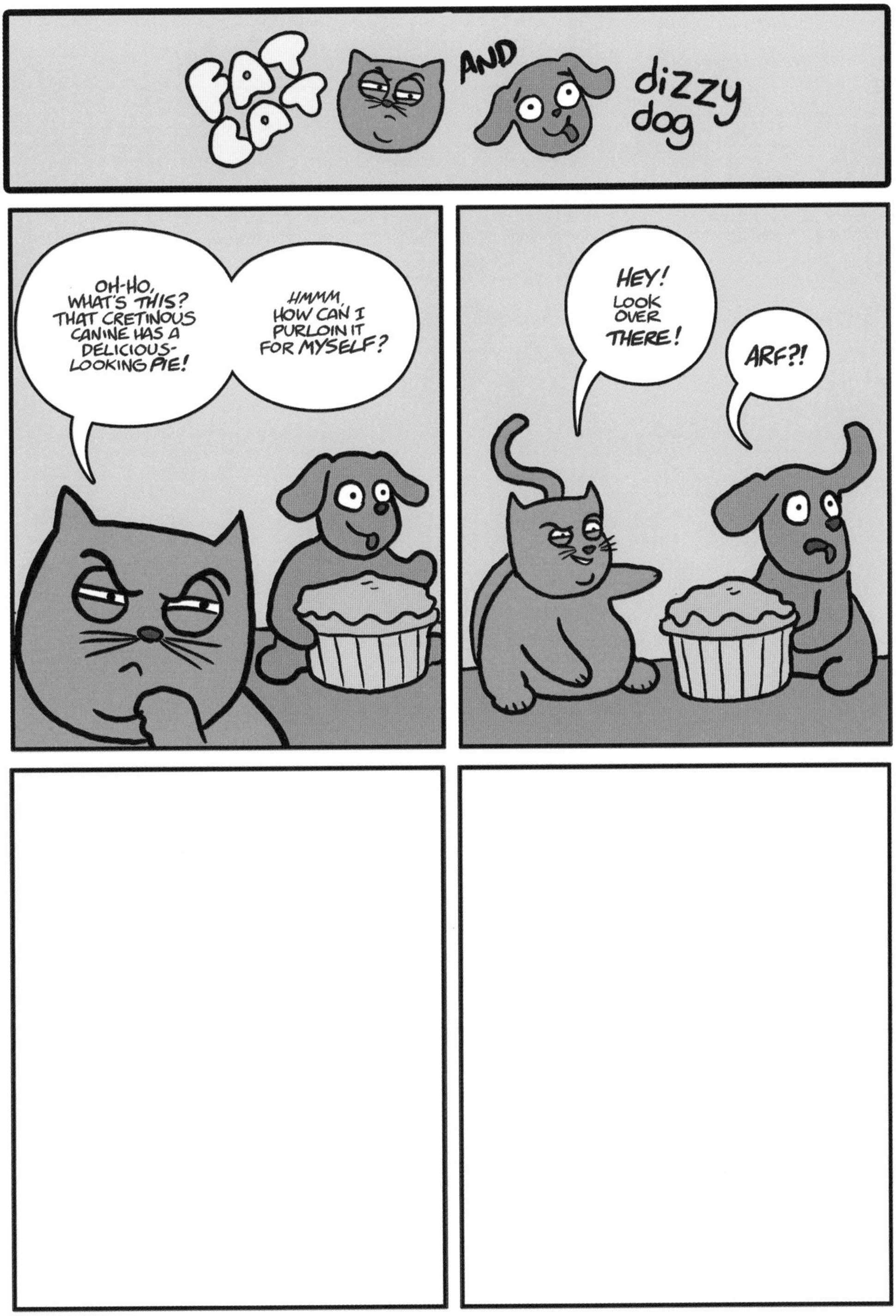
FAT CAT AND dizzy dog
OH-HO, WHAT'S THIS? THAT CRETINOUS CANINE HAS A DELICIOUS-LOOKING PIE!
HMMM, HOW CAN I PURLOIN IT FOR MYSELF?
HEY! LOOK OVER THERE!
ARF?!

LESSON 2:

(AWESOME) COMICS CAN BE ABOUT ANYTHING

SO! TIME TO TALK ABOUT WHAT COMICS ARE *ABOUT.*

NOW, A LOT OF COMICS YOU SEE IN THE STORES ARE ABOUT SUPERHEROES, ROBOTS... THAT KIND OF THING.

THUMP SQUAD

TASMANIAN DEVIL MAN

ROBOT ACTION

THERE'S NOTHING WRONG WITH ALL THAT STUFF. LET'S BE CLEAR: ROBOTS AND SUPERHEROES ARE AWESOME.

BUT YOU CAN MAKE A COOL COMIC ABOUT ABSOLUTELY *ANYTHING!*

FOR EXAMPLE: WHAT ARE YOU GUYS INTO? WHAT ARE YOUR FAVORITE THINGS?

SOCCER!

BALLET!!

UM... ASTRONOMY?

YOU HEARD 'EM, ART MONKEY. GET TO WORK!

OOK!

EEK.

...SO WHY NOT MAKE COMICS ABOUT THE THINGS *YOU* LOVE?

OOH!

AMAZING SOCCER ACTION

YAY!

tragic Ballet tales!

SOB!

THRILLING ASTRONOMY COMICS

IN THIS ISSUE: PLANETS!

AWESOME!

OR WHY NOT GET TOGETHER WITH SOME FRIENDS AND MIX IT UP A BIT?

OOOK!

THRILLING ASTRONOMICAL BALLETIC SOCCER TALES

HOLE

COOL!

SWEET!

I LIKE HIS *TUTU.*

ART MONKEY CHALLENGE!

OOK!*

COMICS

* OKAY, GU[...] YOUR TU[...]

TRY DESIG[...] A LOGO A[...] DRAWING [...] COVER FO[...] COMIC AB[...] SOMETHI[...] YOU LOV[...]

KUNG-FU[...] ROMAN[...] HISTORY[...] FLOWER[...] ARRANGIN[...] IT'S UP T[...] YOU!

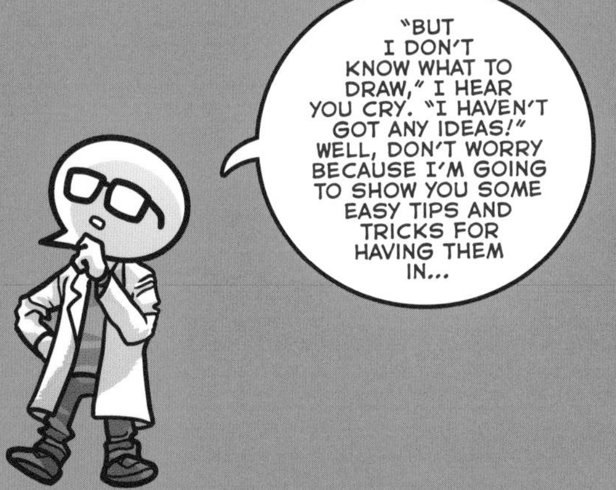
"BUT I DON'T KNOW WHAT TO DRAW," I HEAR YOU CRY. "I HAVEN'T GOT ANY IDEAS!" WELL, DON'T WORRY BECAUSE I'M GOING TO SHOW YOU SOME EASY TIPS AND TRICKS FOR HAVING THEM IN...

CHAPTER 2

HOW TO HAVE (AWESOME) IDEAS

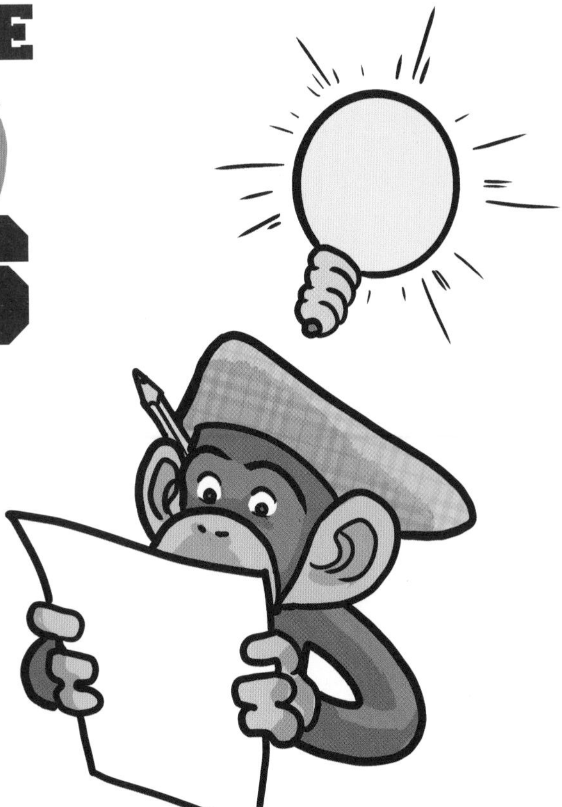

LESSON 3: HOW TO HAVE (AWESOME) IDEAS

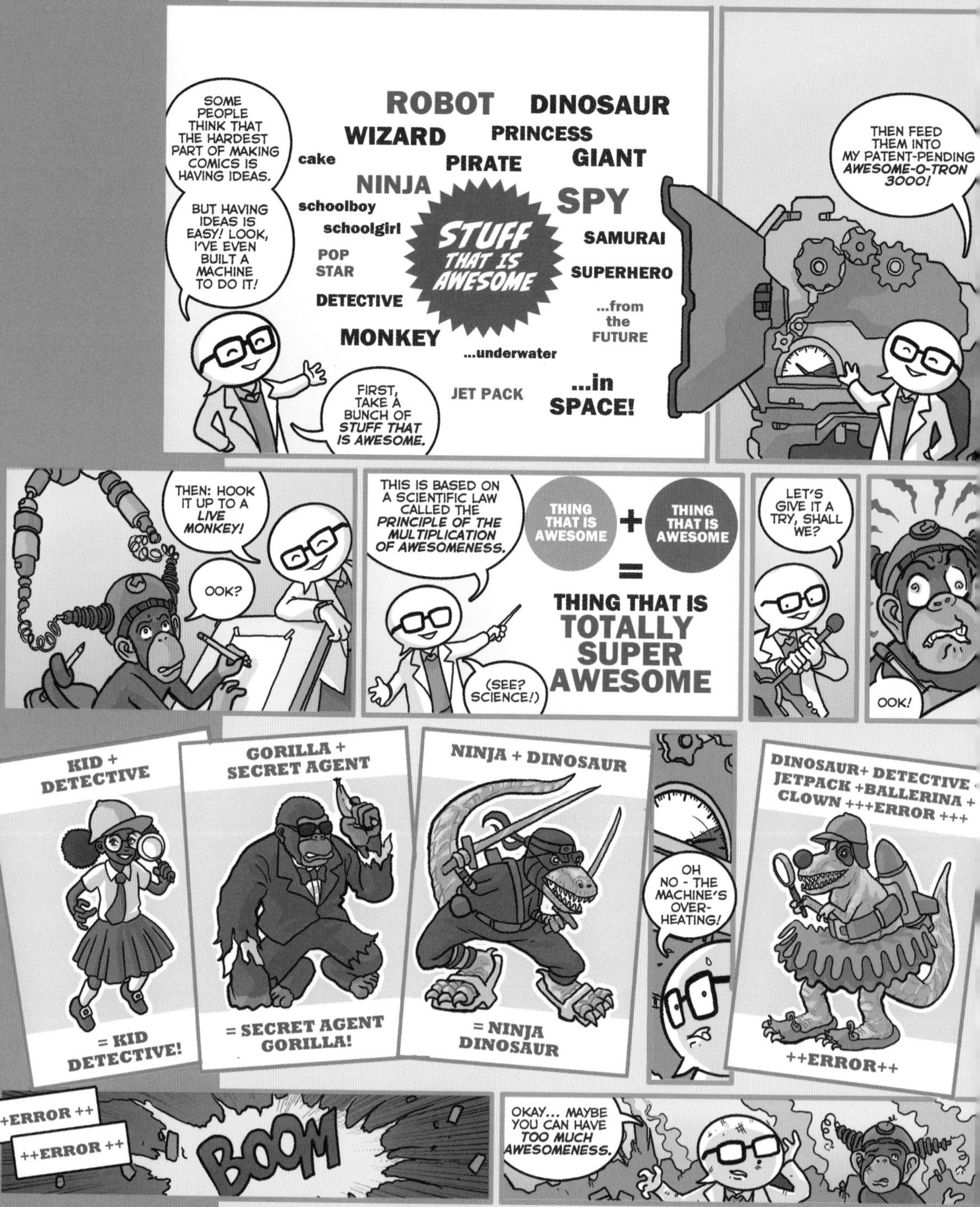

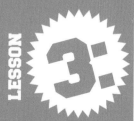

SOME PEOPLE THINK THAT THE HARDEST PART OF MAKING COMICS IS HAVING IDEAS.
BUT HAVING IDEAS IS EASY! LOOK, I'VE EVEN BUILT A MACHINE TO DO IT!
ROBOT
DINOSAUR
WIZARD
PRINCESS
cake
PIRATE
GIANT
NINJA
SPY
schoolboy
schoolgirl
STUFF THAT IS AWESOME
SAMURAI
POP STAR
SUPERHERO
DETECTIVE
...from the FUTURE
MONKEY
...underwater
JET PACK
...in SPACE!
FIRST, TAKE A BUNCH OF STUFF THAT IS AWESOME.
THEN FEED THEM INTO MY PATENT-PENDING AWESOME-O-TRON 3000!
THEN: HOOK IT UP TO A LIVE MONKEY!
OOK?
THIS IS BASED ON A SCIENTIFIC LAW CALLED THE PRINCIPLE OF THE MULTIPLICATION OF AWESOMENESS.
THING THAT IS AWESOME + THING THAT IS AWESOME = THING THAT IS TOTALLY SUPER AWESOME
(SEE? SCIENCE!)
LET'S GIVE IT A TRY, SHALL WE?
OOK!
KID + DETECTIVE
= KID DETECTIVE!
GORILLA + SECRET AGENT
= SECRET AGENT GORILLA!
NINJA + DINOSAUR
= NINJA DINOSAUR
OH NO - THE MACHINE'S OVER-HEATING!
DINOSAUR+ DETECTIVE + JETPACK +BALLERINA + CLOWN +++ERROR +++
++ERROR++
++ERROR ++
++ERROR ++
BOOM
OKAY... MAYBE YOU CAN HAVE TOO MUCH AWESOMENESS.

ART MONKEY CHALLENGE!

 OOK!*

* OKAY, TIME TO CREATE YOUR OWN AWESOME NEW COMIC CHARACTER!

JUST USE THIS HANDY FORMULA AND AWAY YOU GO!

 THING THAT IS AWESOME #1:

+

 =

 THING THAT IS AWESOME #2:

NEED SOME IDEAS? HOW ABOUT...

FIG. A: SOME THINGS THAT ARE AWESOME

PIRATE

ROBOT

DINOSAUR

NINJA

MERMAID

ALIEN

KID

MONKEY

APPENDIX ALERT — TURN TO PAGES 57+61

THERE ARE LOADS MORE CHARACTERS FOR YOU TO MIX UP IN APPENDIX A, PLUS SOME CRAZY PENGUINS IN APPENDIX F!

LESSON 4: HOW TO HAVE (AWESOMER) IDEAS

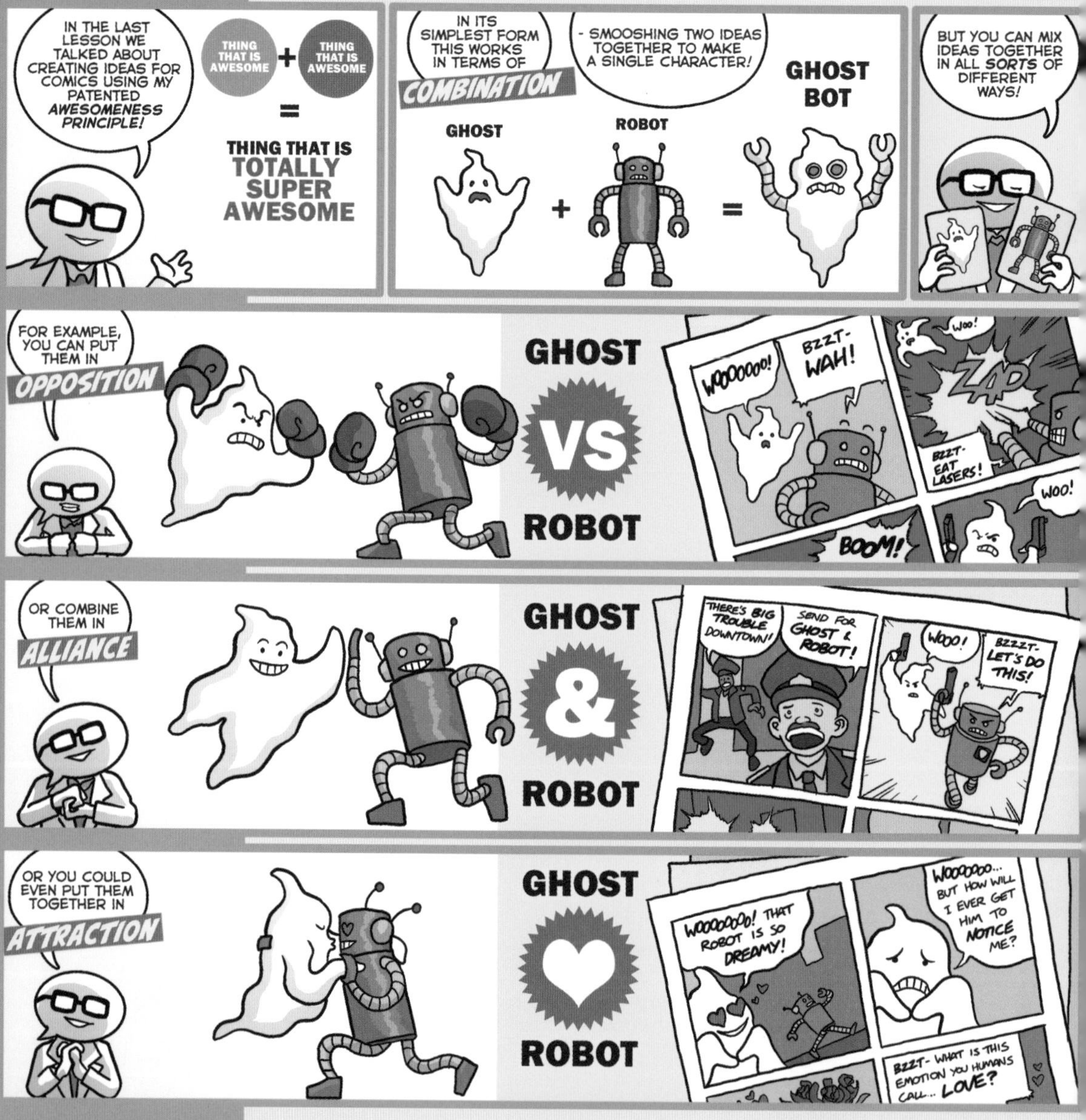

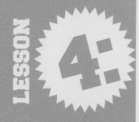

IN THE LAST LESSON WE TALKED ABOUT CREATING IDEAS FOR COMICS USING MY PATENTED AWESOMENESS PRINCIPLE!
THING THAT IS AWESOME + THING THAT IS AWESOME = THING THAT IS TOTALLY SUPER AWESOME
IN ITS SIMPLEST FORM THIS WORKS IN TERMS OF
COMBINATION
- SMOOSHING TWO IDEAS TOGETHER TO MAKE A SINGLE CHARACTER!
GHOST + ROBOT = GHOST BOT
BUT YOU CAN MIX IDEAS TOGETHER IN ALL SORTS OF DIFFERENT WAYS!
FOR EXAMPLE, YOU CAN PUT THEM IN
OPPOSITION
GHOST VS ROBOT
WOOOOOO!
BZZT-WAH!
WOO!
ZAP
BZZT-EAT LASERS!
WOO!
BOOM!
OR COMBINE THEM IN
ALLIANCE
GHOST & ROBOT
THERE'S BIG TROUBLE DOWNTOWN!
SEND FOR GHOST & ROBOT!
WOOO!
BZZZT-LET'S DO THIS!
OR YOU COULD EVEN PUT THEM TOGETHER IN
ATTRACTION
GHOST ♥ ROBOT
WOOOOOOO! THAT ROBOT IS SO DREAMY!
WOOOOOOO... BUT HOW WILL I EVER GET HIM TO NOTICE ME?
BZZT- WHAT IS THIS EMOTION YOU HUMANS CALL... LOVE?

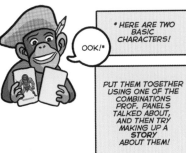

RT MONKEY CHALLENGE!

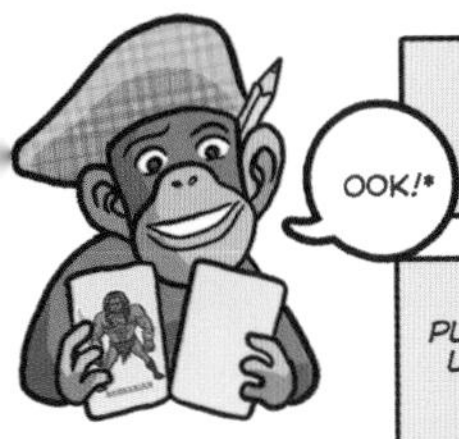

OOK!*

* HERE ARE TWO BASIC CHARACTERS!

PUT THEM TOGETHER USING ONE OF THE COMBINATIONS PROF. PANELS TALKED ABOUT, AND THEN TRY MAKING UP A **STORY** ABOUT THEM!

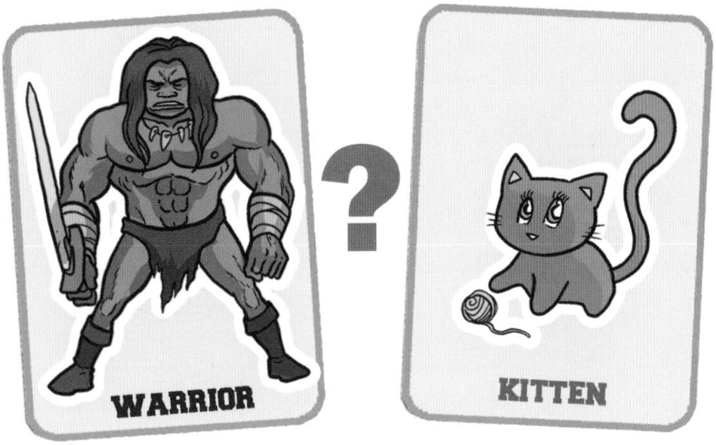

WARRIOR
?
KITTEN

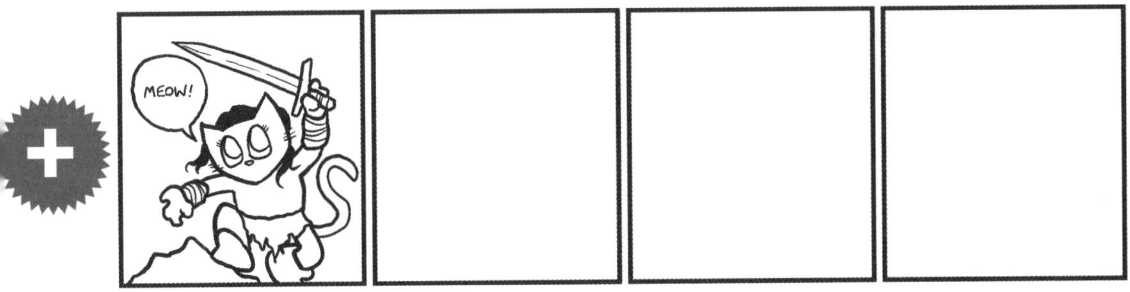

+
MEOW!

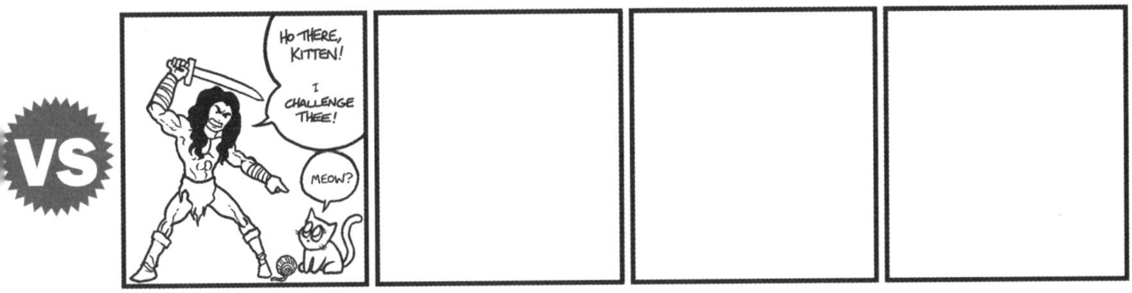

VS
HO THERE, KITTEN!
I CHALLENGE THEE!
MEOW?

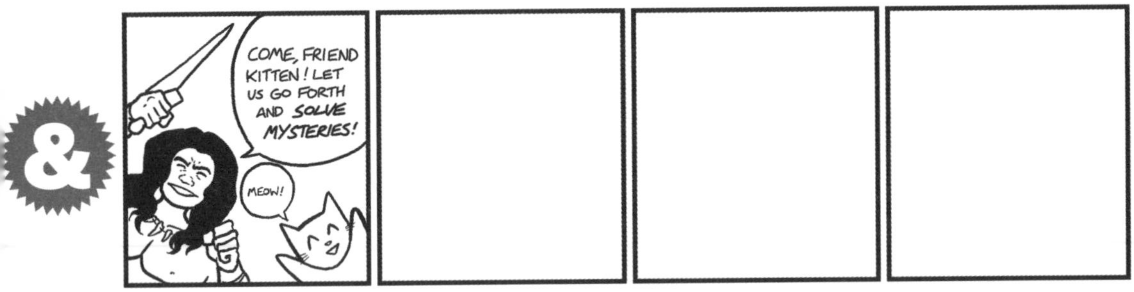

&
COME, FRIEND KITTEN! LET US GO FORTH AND SOLVE MYSTERIES!
MEOW!

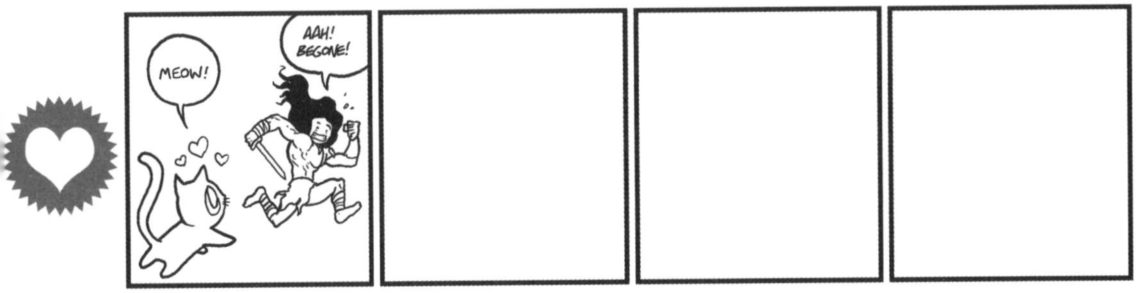

MEOW!
AAH! BEGONE!

Panel 1: BY NOW YOU SHOULD HAVE THE HANG OF MY *AWESOMENESS PRINCIPLE* —

— AND HOW IT'S THE PERFECT WAY TO COME UP WITH IDEAS FOR COMICS!

THING THAT IS AWESOME + THING THAT IS AWESOME = **THING THAT IS TOTALLY SUPER AWESOME**

Panel 2: IT'S NOT *JUST* A FUN, COOL EXCUSE TO DRAW MASH-UP CHARACTERS LIKE *NINJA WOMBATS* AND SUCHLIKE...

(ALTHOUGH NINJA WOMBATS *ARE* COOL.)

GRRRR...

Panel 3: IT'S REALLY ABOUT USING THE GENIUS WAY YOUR BRAIN WORKS — TO MAKE AMAZING *NEW* COMICS!

Panel 4: EVEN WHEN WE'RE REALLY TINY, OUR BRAINS ARE DOING AMAZING STUFF — SPOTTING THE DIFFERENT *ELEMENTS* AND *IDEAS* THAT MAKE UP ALL THE THINGS AROUND US.

Panel 5: WE SOON FIGURE OUT WHICH THINGS GO NATURALLY TOGETHER...

Panel 6: BUT OUR BRAINS ALSO STORE ALL THOSE IDEAS AND ELEMENTS *SEPARATELY* — READY FOR US TO *SMOOSH* 'EM TOGETHER IN COOL NEW WAYS THAT DON'T YET EXIST IN THE WORLD!

Panel 7: AND READING BOOKS AND COMICS ADDS EVEN MORE TO THE MIX — FILLING YOUR HEAD WITH IDEAS AND CONCEPTS AND *GENERAL AWESOMENESS!*

Panel 8: WHICH GIVES YOU EVEN MORE RAW MATERIAL TO *SMOOSH TOGETHER* IN AWESOME NEW WAYS!

Panel 9: AND IT'S OFTEN BY COMBINING YOUR *FAVORITE* THINGS — THE THINGS *YOU* LOVE MOST OF ALL —

Panel 10: — THAT YOU'LL FIND YOU'VE SMOOSHED TOGETHER ELEMENTS THAT NOBODY EVER THOUGHT TO SMOOSH BEFORE...

Panel 11: ...AND THOSE ARE THE *AWESOMEST IDEAS OF ALL!*

CHECK IT OUT, I MADE A COMIC ABOUT WRESTLERS...

...WHO ARE ZOMBIES!

SWEET!

ART MONKEY CHALLENGE!

OOK!*

*NOW IT'S YOUR TURN! WE'RE GOING TO TRY PUTTING TWO CONCEPTS TOGETHER AGAIN - BUT THIS TIME, USING THINGS PERSONAL TO YOU, TO TRY AND CREATE SOMETHING UNIQUELY AWESOME!

MY FAVORITE THING IN THE WHOLE WORLD:

+

MY (SECOND) FAVORITE THING IN THE WHOLE WORLD:

=

EXAMPLE:
(by Art Monkey)

MY FAVORITE THING IN THE WHOLE WORLD:

BANANAS

+

MY (SECOND) FAVORITE THING IN THE WHOLE WORLD:

BALLET

=

BANANARINA!

LESSON 6: REAL LIFE (AWESOME

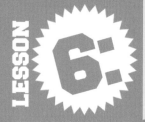

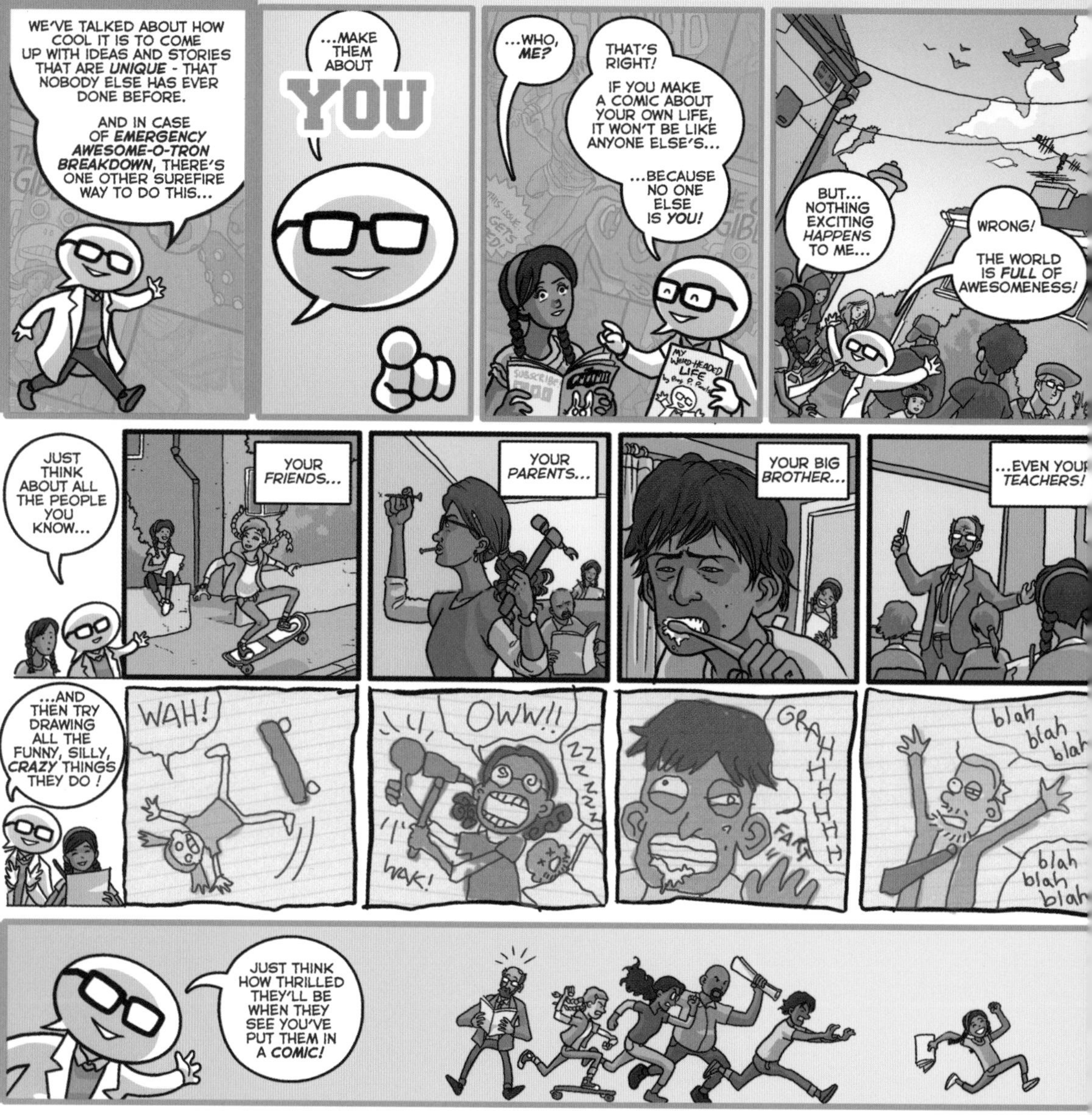
WE'VE TALKED ABOUT HOW COOL IT IS TO COME UP WITH IDEAS AND STORIES THAT ARE *UNIQUE* - THAT NOBODY ELSE HAS EVER DONE BEFORE.
AND IN CASE OF ***EMERGENCY AWESOME-O-TRON BREAKDOWN***, THERE'S ONE OTHER SUREFIRE WAY TO DO THIS...
...MAKE THEM ABOUT
YOU
...WHO, *ME?*
THAT'S RIGHT!
IF YOU MAKE A COMIC ABOUT YOUR OWN LIFE, IT WON'T BE LIKE ANYONE ELSE'S...
...BECAUSE NO ONE ELSE IS *YOU!*
MY WEIRD-HEADED LIFE
BUT... NOTHING EXCITING *HAPPENS* TO ME...
WRONG!
THE WORLD IS *FULL* OF AWESOMENESS!
JUST THINK ABOUT ALL THE PEOPLE YOU KNOW...
YOUR FRIENDS...
YOUR PARENTS...
YOUR BIG BROTHER...
...EVEN YOUR TEACHERS!
...AND THEN TRY DRAWING ALL THE FUNNY, SILLY, *CRAZY* THINGS THEY DO!
WAH!
OWW!!
ZZZZZ
WAK!
GRAHHHHHHH
FART
blah blah blah
blah blah blah
JUST THINK HOW THRILLED THEY'LL BE WHEN THEY SEE YOU'VE PUT THEM IN A *COMIC!*

ART MONKEY CHALLENGE!

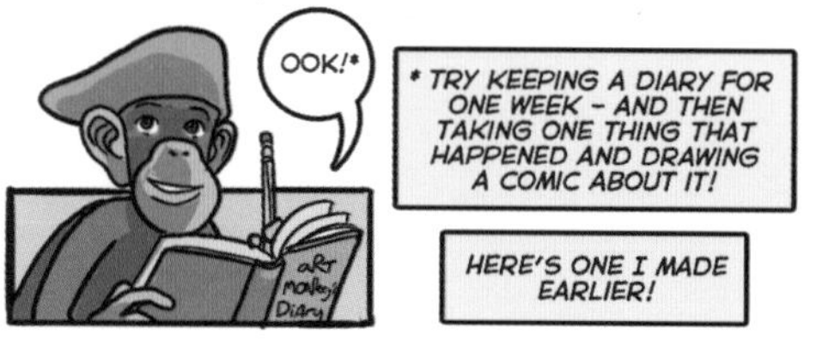
OOK!*
* TRY KEEPING A DIARY FOR ONE WEEK - AND THEN TAKING ONE THING THAT HAPPENED AND DRAWING A COMIC ABOUT IT!
HERE'S ONE I MADE EARLIER!
ART MONKEY DIARY

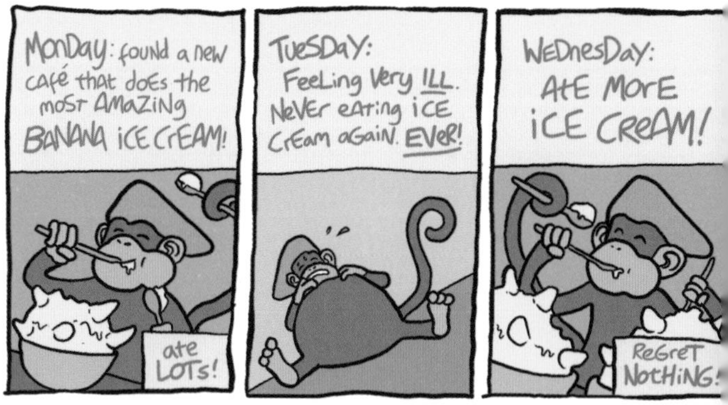
MONDAY: found a new café that does the most AMAZING BANANA ICE CREAM!
ate LOTS!
TUESDAY: Feeling very ILL. Never eating ice cream again. EVER!
WEDNESDAY: ATE MORE ICE CREAM!
REGRET NOTHING!

NOW THAT YOU KNOW ALL ABOUT HOW TO HAVE GREAT IDEAS, I BET YOU WANT TO START TURNING THOSE IDEAS INTO AWESOME COMICS! FIRST, IT'S TIME FOR YOU ALL TO BECOME SUPER-COMICS EXPERTS, WITH...

CHAPTER 3

HOW (AWESOME) COMICS WORK

LESSON 7: HOW (AWESOME) COMICS WORK

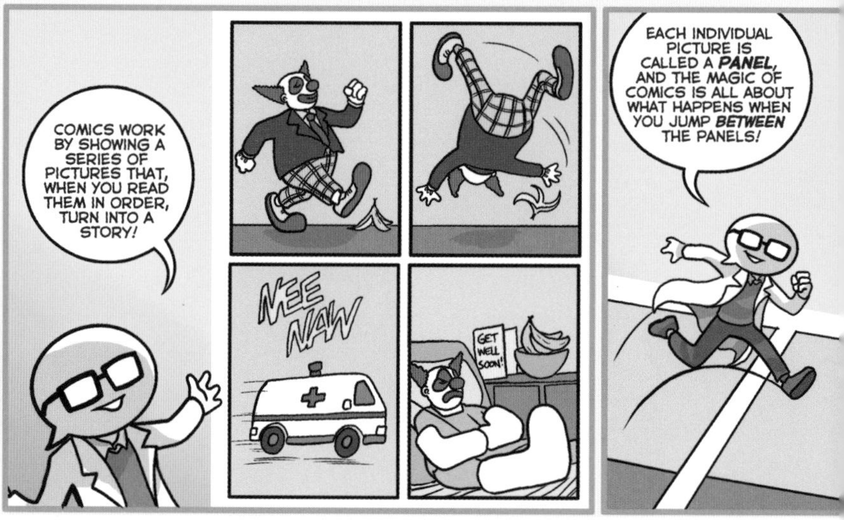
COMICS WORK BY SHOWING A SERIES OF PICTURES THAT, WHEN YOU READ THEM IN ORDER, TURN INTO A STORY!
NEE NAW
GET WELL SOON!
EACH INDIVIDUAL PICTURE IS CALLED A **PANEL**, AND THE MAGIC OF COMICS IS ALL ABOUT WHAT HAPPENS WHEN YOU JUMP ***BETWEEN*** THE PANELS!

YOU CAN SHOW AN ACTION IN ONE PANEL LEADING DIRECTLY TO A REACTION IN THE NEXT!

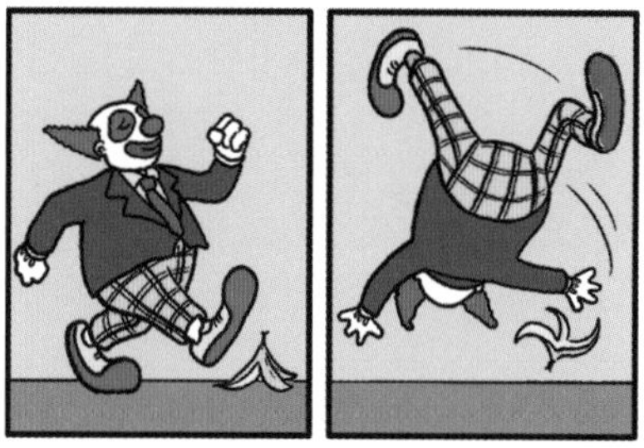

BUT THAT'S NOT THE ONLY WAY YOU CAN TELL THE STORY. YOU ***COULD*** JUMP FORWARD IN TIME:

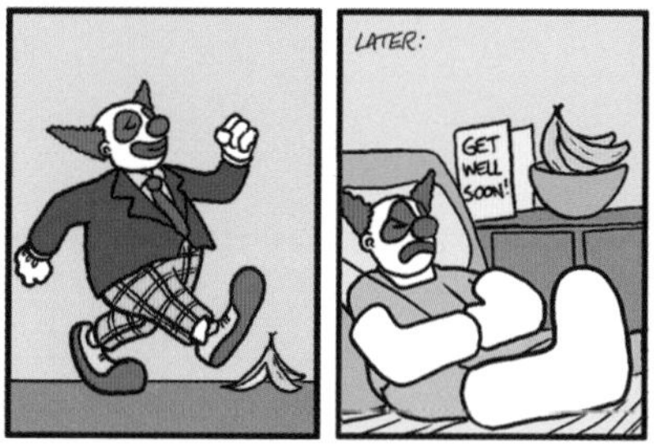
LATER:
GET WELL SOON!

OR YOU COULD JUMP ***BACK*** IN TIME, SHOWING WHAT HAPPENED EARLIER . . .

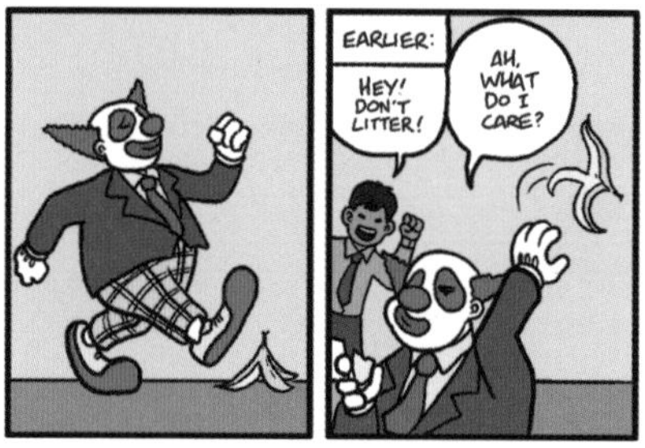
EARLIER:
HEY! DON'T LITTER!
AH, WHAT DO I CARE?

YOU CAN CHANGE SCENE, TO SHOW WHAT'S HAPPENING SOMEWHERE ELSE...

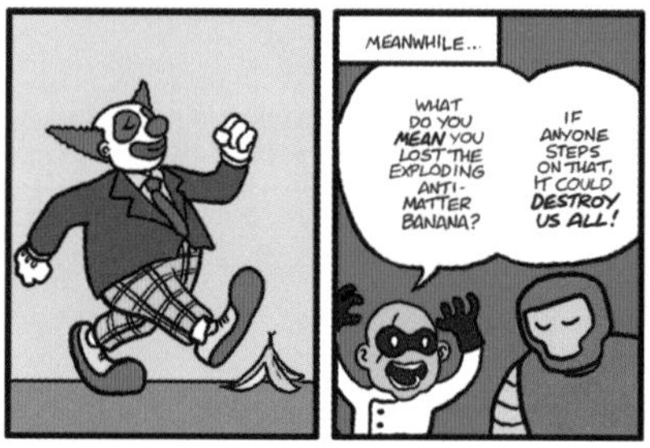
MEANWHILE...
WHAT DO YOU ***MEAN*** YOU LOST THE EXPLODING ANTI-MATTER BANANA?
IF ANYONE STEPS ON THAT, IT COULD ***DESTROY US ALL!***

YOU CAN ZOOM IN AND SHOW THE DETAIL OF WHAT'S HAPPENING, TO SLOW DOWN THE ACTION AND BUILD TENSION...

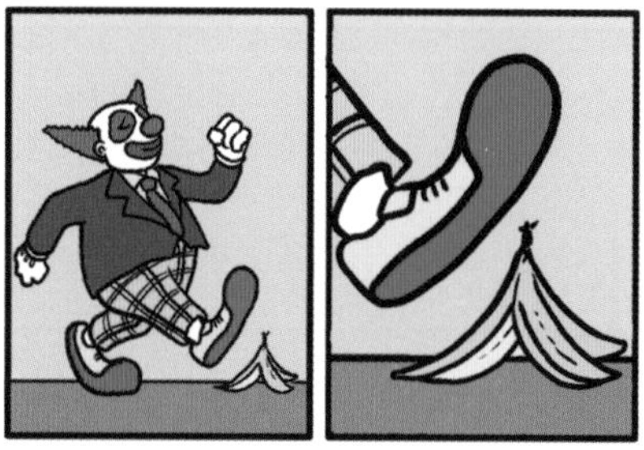

OR ZOOM OUT, TO SHOW A WIDER VIEW OF THE SCENE...

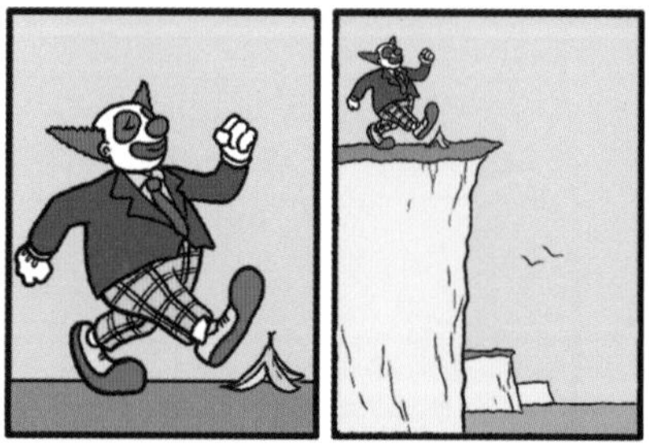

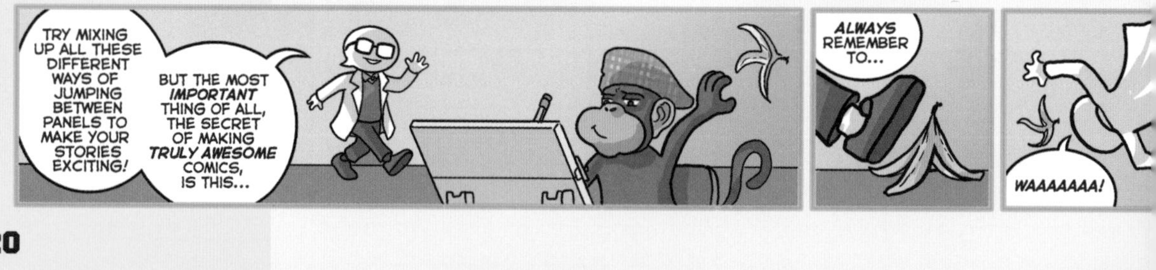
TRY MIXING UP ALL THESE DIFFERENT WAYS OF JUMPING BETWEEN PANELS TO MAKE YOUR STORIES EXCITING!
BUT THE MOST ***IMPORTANT*** THING OF ALL, THE SECRET OF MAKING ***TRULY AWESOME*** COMICS, IS THIS...
ALWAYS REMEMBER TO...
WAAAAAAA!

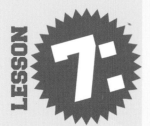

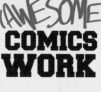

ART MONKEY CHALLENGE!

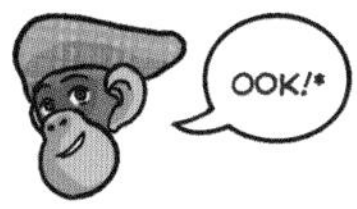

OOK!*

* OKAY, GUYS, YOUR TURN! HERE'S A COMIC STRIP WITH HALF THE PANELS LEFT BLANK! FILL THEM IN TO FINISH THE STORY, USING SOME OF THE TRICKS PROF. P WAS TALKING ABOUT!

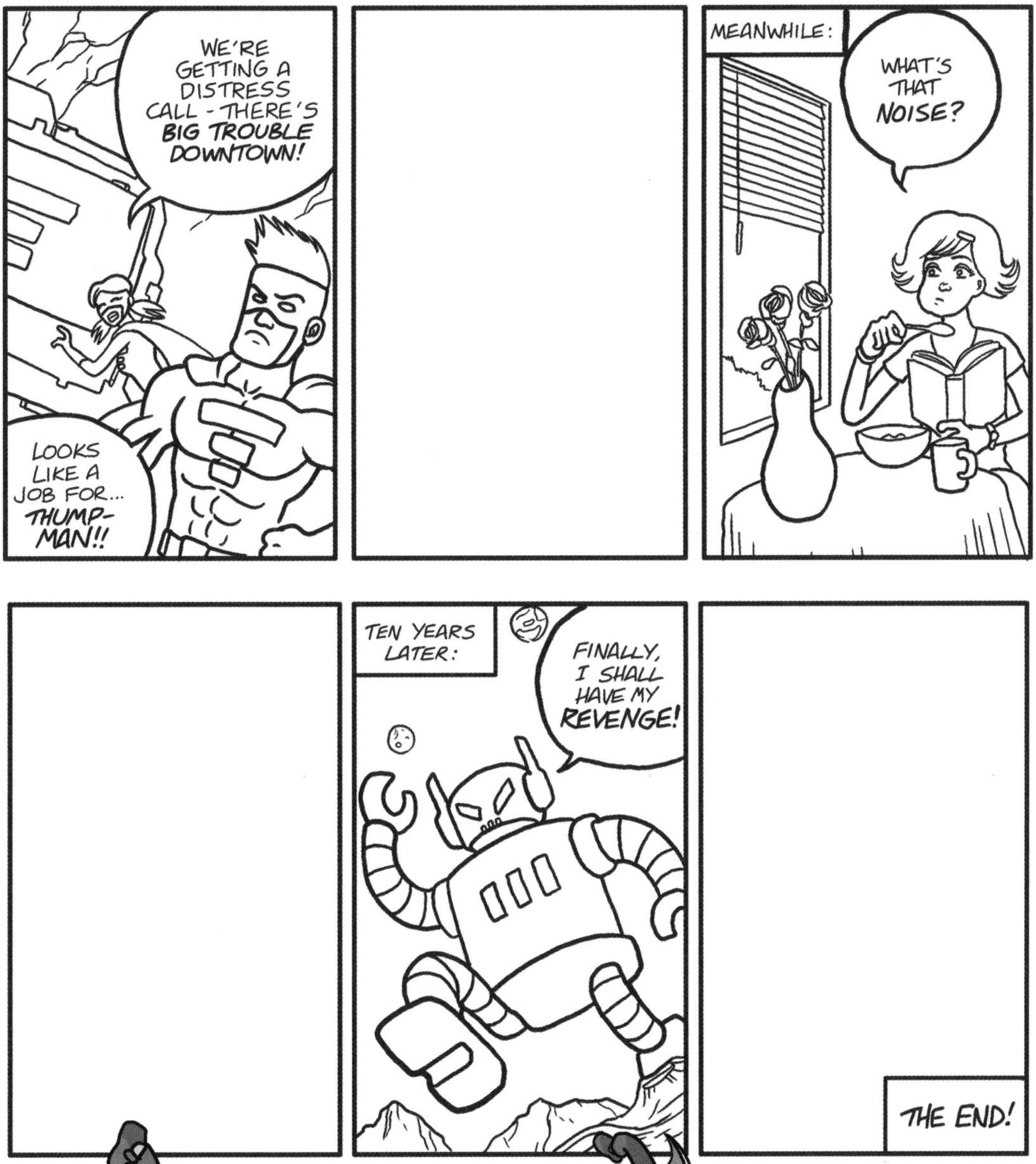

WE'RE GETTING A DISTRESS CALL - THERE'S BIG TROUBLE DOWNTOWN!
LOOKS LIKE A JOB FOR... THUMP-MAN!!
MEANWHILE:
WHAT'S THAT NOISE?
TEN YEARS LATER:
FINALLY, I SHALL HAVE MY REVENGE!
THE END!

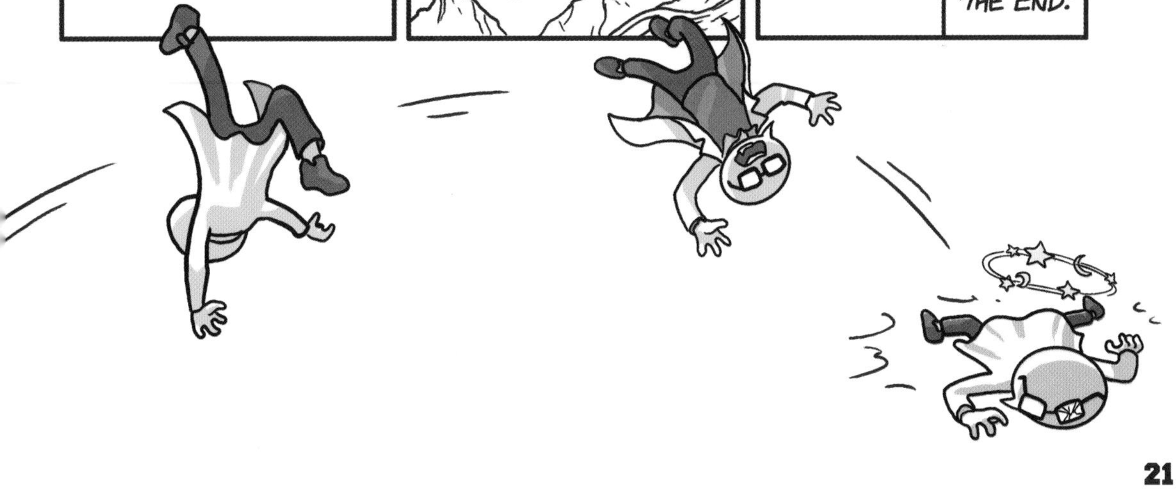

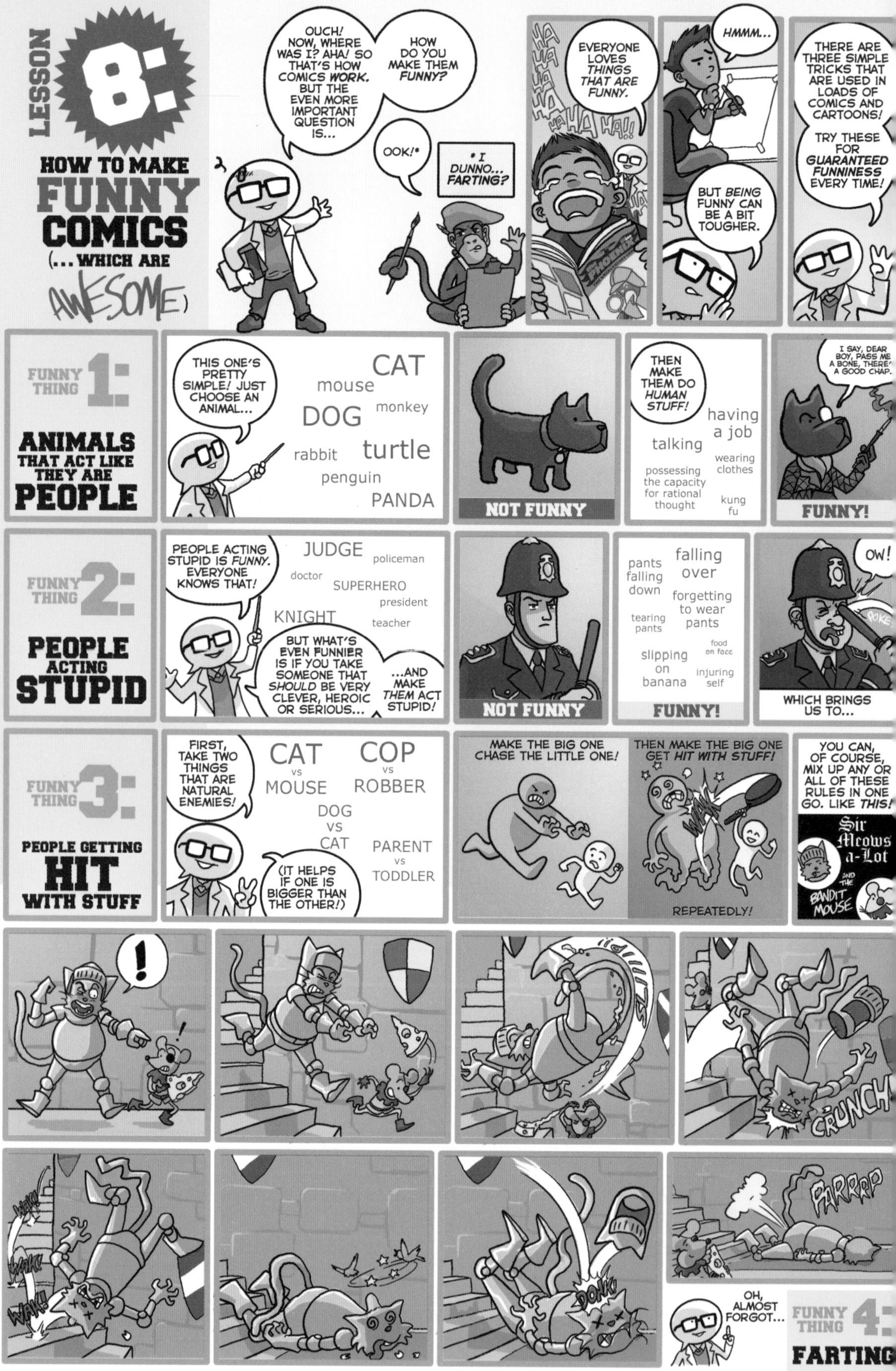
LESSON 8:
HOW TO MAKE FUNNY COMICS (... WHICH ARE AWESOME)
OUCH! NOW, WHERE WAS I? AHA! SO THAT'S HOW COMICS WORK. BUT THE EVEN MORE IMPORTANT QUESTION IS...
HOW DO YOU MAKE THEM FUNNY?
OOK!*
* I DUNNO... FARTING?
EVERYONE LOVES THINGS THAT ARE FUNNY.
HA HA HA HA HA!!
PHOENIX
HMMM...
BUT BEING FUNNY CAN BE A BIT TOUGHER.
THERE ARE THREE SIMPLE TRICKS THAT ARE USED IN LOADS OF COMICS AND CARTOONS!
TRY THESE FOR GUARANTEED FUNNINESS EVERY TIME!
FUNNY THING 1: ANIMALS THAT ACT LIKE THEY ARE PEOPLE
THIS ONE'S PRETTY SIMPLE! JUST CHOOSE AN ANIMAL...
CAT
mouse
monkey
DOG
rabbit
turtle
penguin
PANDA
NOT FUNNY
THEN MAKE THEM DO HUMAN STUFF!
having a job
talking
wearing clothes
possessing the capacity for rational thought
kung fu
I SAY, DEAR BOY, PASS ME A BONE, THERE'S A GOOD CHAP.
FUNNY!
FUNNY THING 2: PEOPLE ACTING STUPID
PEOPLE ACTING STUPID IS FUNNY. EVERYONE KNOWS THAT!
JUDGE
policeman
doctor
SUPERHERO
president
KNIGHT
teacher
BUT WHAT'S EVEN FUNNIER IS IF YOU TAKE SOMEONE THAT SHOULD BE VERY CLEVER, HEROIC OR SERIOUS...
...AND MAKE THEM ACT STUPID!
NOT FUNNY
pants falling down
falling over
forgetting to wear pants
tearing pants
food on face
slipping on banana
injuring self
FUNNY!
OW!
POKE
WHICH BRINGS US TO...
FUNNY THING 3: PEOPLE GETTING HIT WITH STUFF
FIRST, TAKE TWO THINGS THAT ARE NATURAL ENEMIES!
CAT vs MOUSE
COP vs ROBBER
DOG vs CAT
PARENT vs TODDLER
(IT HELPS IF ONE IS BIGGER THAN THE OTHER!)
MAKE THE BIG ONE CHASE THE LITTLE ONE!
THEN MAKE THE BIG ONE GET HIT WITH STUFF!
WHAK
REPEATEDLY!
YOU CAN, OF COURSE, MIX UP ANY OR ALL OF THESE RULES IN ONE GO. LIKE THIS!
Sir Meows a-Lot AND THE BANDIT MOUSE
!
!
CRUNCH
WAK!
WAK!
WAK!
DONK!
FARRRP
OH, ALMOST FORGOT...
FUNNY THING 4: FARTING

ART MONKEY CHALLENGE!

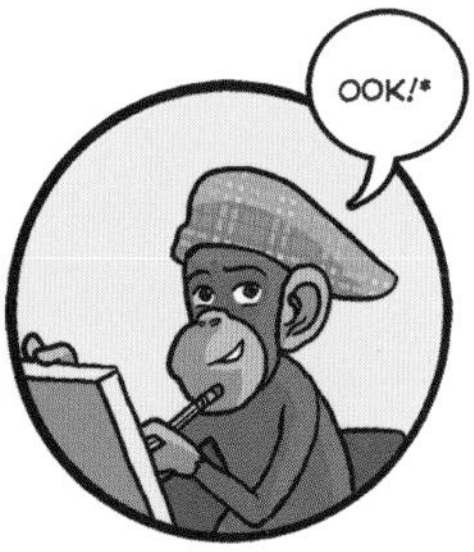

OOK!*

* OKAY, GUYS, IT'S YOUR TURN!

TRY USING THESE THREE SIMPLE TECHNIQUES BASED ON THE PROF'S LESSON FOR SURE-FIRE FUNNINESS!

FUNNINESS TECHNIQUE 1

YOUR FAVORITE ANIMAL:

+

THE JOB YOU'D LIKE TO DO WHEN YOU GROW UP:

NOW DRAW THAT ANIMAL DOING THAT JOB!

BONUS TIP! Some common animals and how to DRAW them:

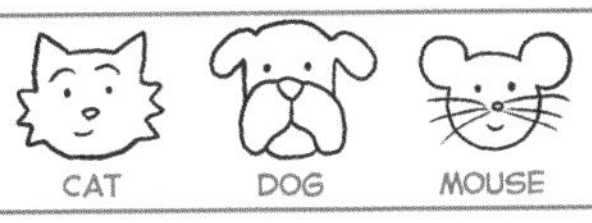

CAT
DOG
MOUSE

FUNNINESS TECHNIQUE 2

THE MOST SERIOUS, IMPORTANT JOB YOU CAN THINK OF:

+ ACTING STUPID

BONUS TIP! How to draw *COMEDY UNDERPANTS!*

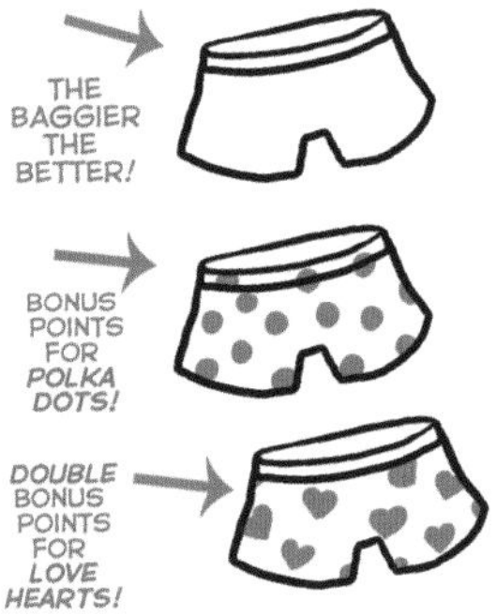

THE BAGGIER THE BETTER!
BONUS POINTS FOR *POLKA DOTS!*
DOUBLE BONUS POINTS FOR *LOVE HEARTS!*

FUNNINESS TECHNIQUE 3

SOMEONE OR SOMETHING THAT IS **BIG:**

+

SOMEONE OR SOMETHING THAT IS **LITTLE:**

BONUS TIP! Some STUFF to have your characters GET HIT WITH:

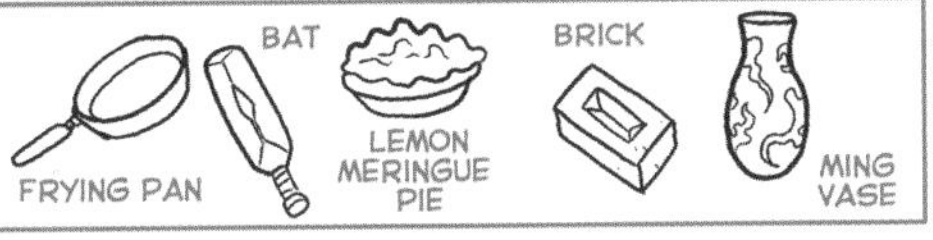

FRYING PAN
BAT
LEMON MERINGUE PIE
BRICK
MING VASE

LESSON 9:

(AWESOME) WORDS + (AWESOME) PICTURES

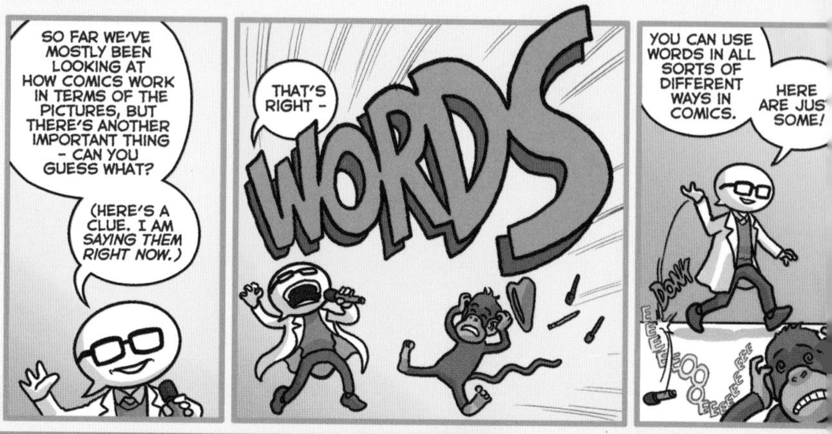

SO FAR WE'VE MOSTLY BEEN LOOKING AT HOW COMICS WORK IN TERMS OF THE PICTURES, BUT THERE'S ANOTHER IMPORTANT THING – CAN YOU GUESS WHAT?
(HERE'S A CLUE. I AM SAYING THEM RIGHT NOW.)
THAT'S RIGHT –
WORDS
YOU CAN USE WORDS IN ALL SORTS OF DIFFERENT WAYS IN COMICS.
HERE ARE JUST SOME!
DONK

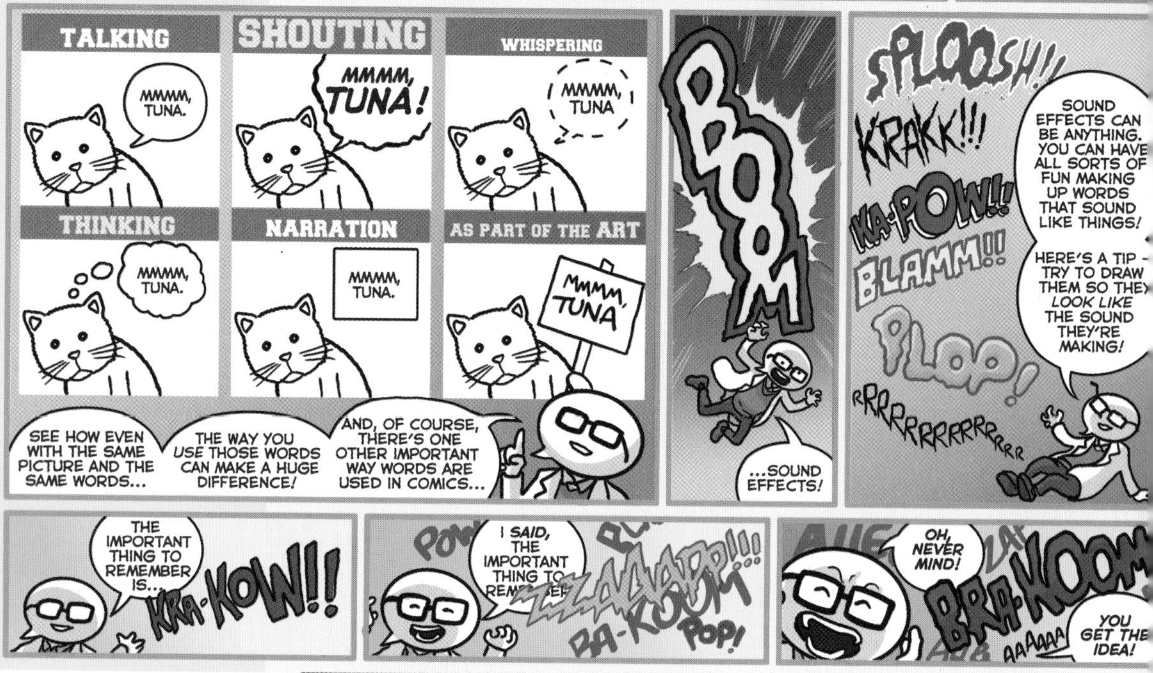

TALKING
MMMM, TUNA.
SHOUTING
MMMM, TUNA!
WHISPERING
MMMM, TUNA
THINKING
MMMM, TUNA.
NARRATION
MMMM, TUNA.
AS PART OF THE ART
MMMM, TUNA
SEE HOW EVEN WITH THE SAME PICTURE AND THE SAME WORDS...
THE WAY YOU USE THOSE WORDS CAN MAKE A HUGE DIFFERENCE!
AND, OF COURSE, THERE'S ONE OTHER IMPORTANT WAY WORDS ARE USED IN COMICS...
BOOM
...SOUND EFFECTS!
SPLOOSH!!
KRAKK!!!
KA-POW!!
BLAMM!!
PLOP!
RRRRRRRRRRRRRRR
SOUND EFFECTS CAN BE ANYTHING. YOU CAN HAVE ALL SORTS OF FUN MAKING UP WORDS THAT SOUND LIKE THINGS!
HERE'S A TIP – TRY TO DRAW THEM SO THEY LOOK LIKE THE SOUND THEY'RE MAKING!
THE IMPORTANT THING TO REMEMBER IS...
KRA-KOW!!
POW
I SAID, THE IMPORTANT THING TO
BA-KOOM
POP!
OH, NEVER MIND!
BRA-KOOM
AAAAAA
YOU GET THE IDEA!

ART MONKEY CHALLENGE!

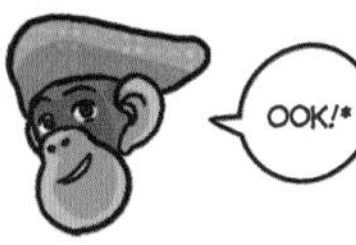

OOK!*

OKAY, GUYS, YOUR TURN! HERE'S A COMIC STRIP WHERE ALL THE WORDS HAVE BEEN LEFT BLANK!

USE ALL THE DIFFERENT TYPES OF SPEECH BUBBLES AND SOUND EFFECTS TO FINISH THE STORY!

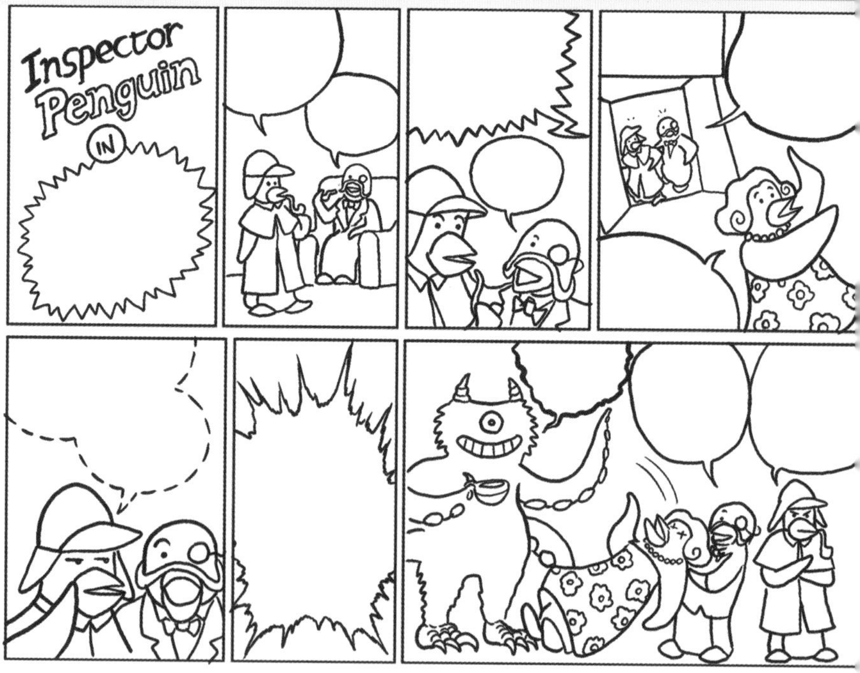

Inspector Penguin
IN

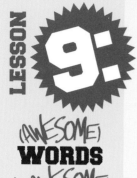

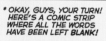

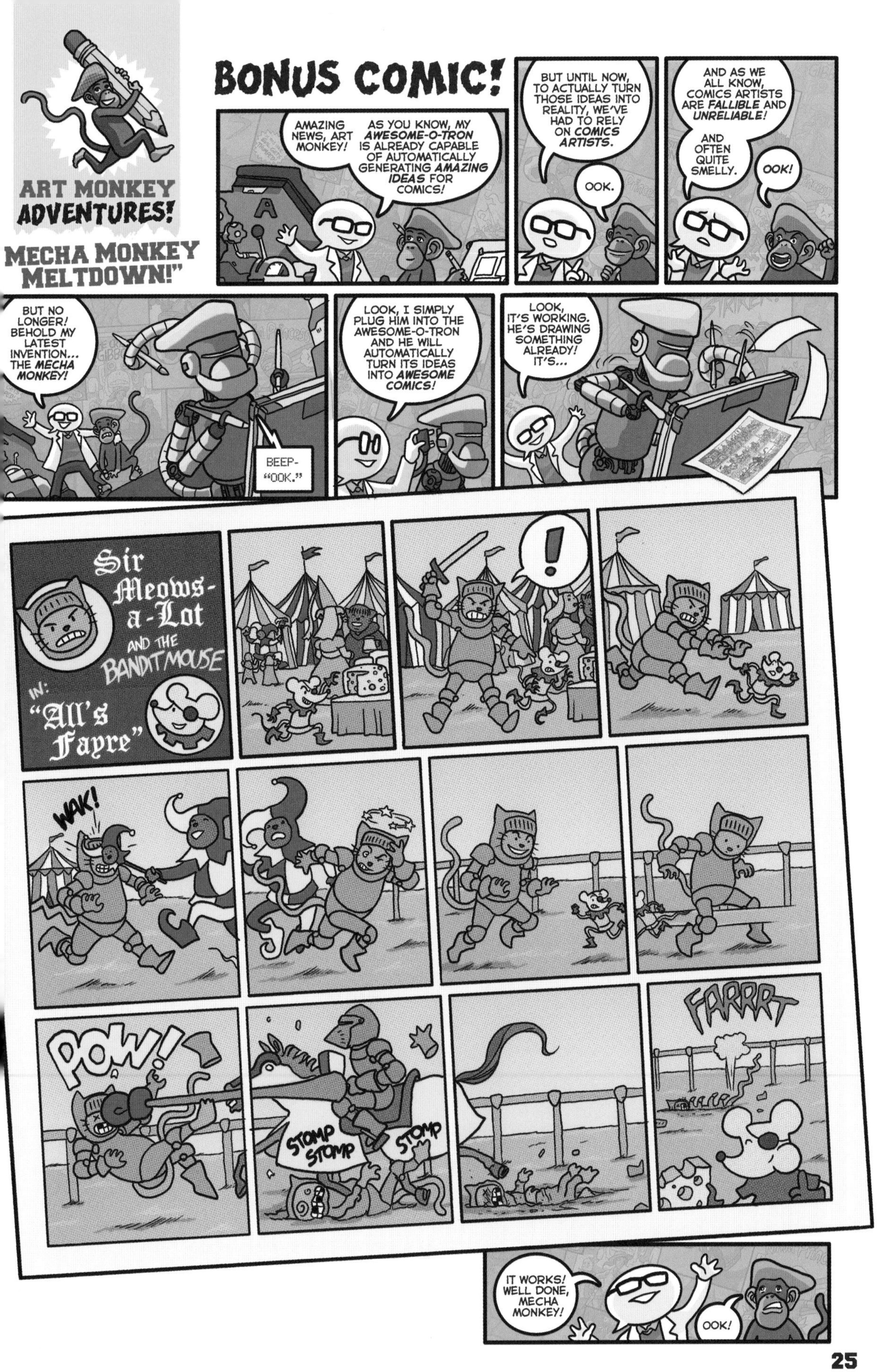
ART MONKEY ADVENTURES!
"MECHA MONKEY MELTDOWN!"
BONUS COMIC!
AMAZING NEWS, ART MONKEY!
AS YOU KNOW, MY AWESOME-O-TRON IS ALREADY CAPABLE OF AUTOMATICALLY GENERATING AMAZING IDEAS FOR COMICS!
BUT UNTIL NOW, TO ACTUALLY TURN THOSE IDEAS INTO REALITY, WE'VE HAD TO RELY ON COMICS ARTISTS.
OOK.
AND AS WE ALL KNOW, COMICS ARTISTS ARE FALLIBLE AND UNRELIABLE!
AND OFTEN QUITE SMELLY.
OOK!
BUT NO LONGER! BEHOLD MY LATEST INVENTION... THE MECHA MONKEY!
BEEP- "OOK."
LOOK, I SIMPLY PLUG HIM INTO THE AWESOME-O-TRON AND HE WILL AUTOMATICALLY TURN ITS IDEAS INTO AWESOME COMICS!
LOOK, IT'S WORKING. HE'S DRAWING SOMETHING ALREADY! IT'S...
Sir Meows-a-Lot
AND THE BANDIT MOUSE
IN: "All's Fayre"
!
WAK!
POW!
STOMP STOMP
STOMP
FARRRT
IT WORKS! WELL DONE, MECHA MONKEY!
OOK!

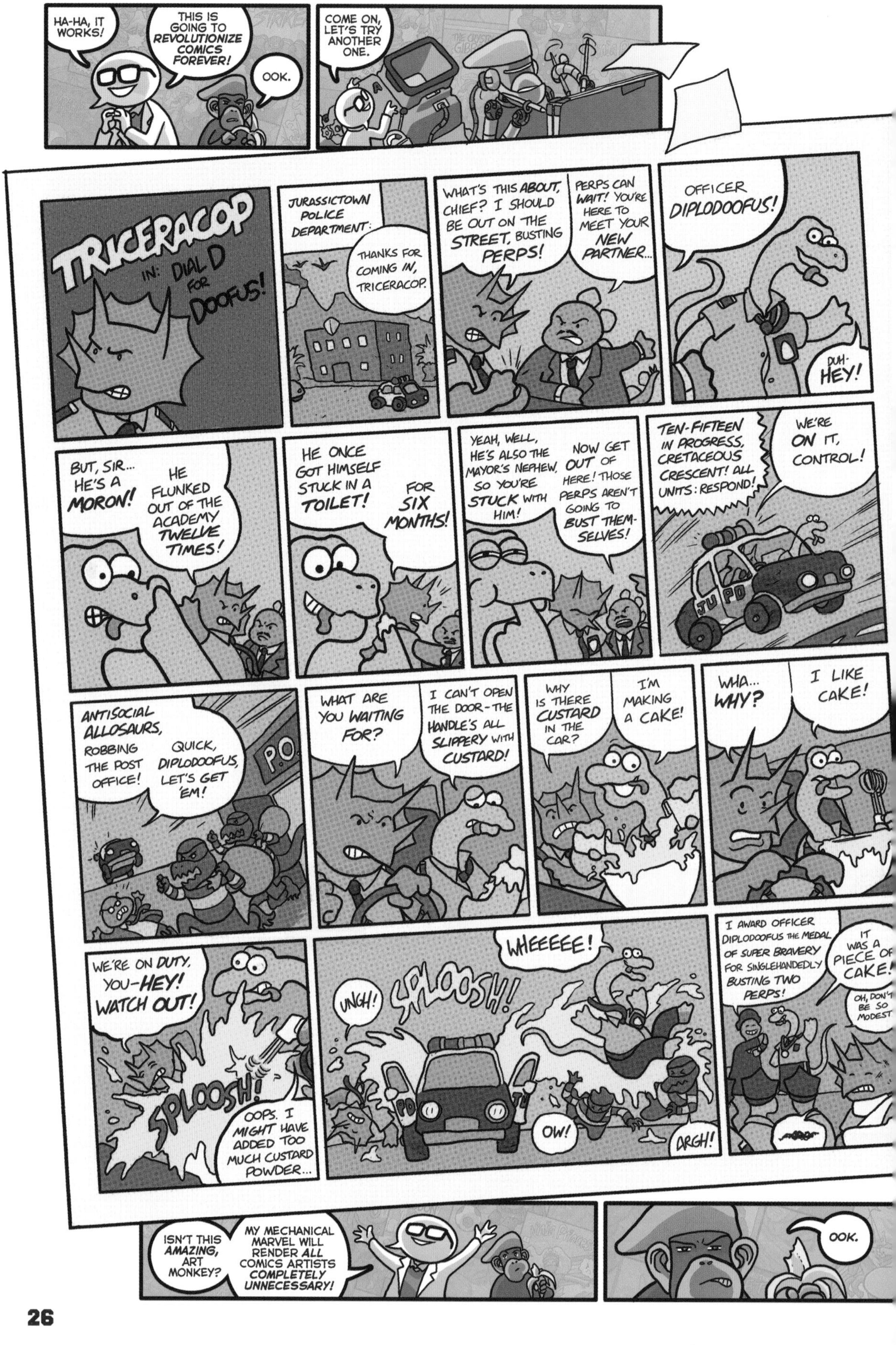

HA-HA, IT WORKS!
THIS IS GOING TO REVOLUTIONIZE COMICS FOREVER!
OOK.
COME ON, LET'S TRY ANOTHER ONE.
TRICERACOP IN: DIAL D FOR DOOFUS!
JURASSICTOWN POLICE DEPARTMENT:
THANKS FOR COMING IN, TRICERACOP.
WHAT'S THIS ABOUT, CHIEF? I SHOULD BE OUT ON THE STREET, BUSTING PERPS!
PERPS CAN WAIT! YOU'RE HERE TO MEET YOUR NEW PARTNER...
OFFICER DIPLODOOFUS!
DUH-HEY!
BUT, SIR... HE'S A MORON!
HE FLUNKED OUT OF THE ACADEMY TWELVE TIMES!
HE ONCE GOT HIMSELF STUCK IN A TOILET!
FOR SIX MONTHS!
YEAH, WELL, HE'S ALSO THE MAYOR'S NEPHEW, SO YOU'RE STUCK WITH HIM!
NOW GET OUT OF HERE! THOSE PERPS AREN'T GOING TO BUST THEMSELVES!
TEN-FIFTEEN IN PROGRESS, CRETACEOUS CRESCENT! ALL UNITS: RESPOND!
WE'RE ON IT, CONTROL!
JU PD
ANTISOCIAL ALLOSAURS, ROBBING THE POST OFFICE!
QUICK, DIPLODOOFUS, LET'S GET 'EM!
P.O.
WHAT ARE YOU WAITING FOR?
I CAN'T OPEN THE DOOR - THE HANDLE'S ALL SLIPPERY WITH CUSTARD!
WHY IS THERE CUSTARD IN THE CAR?
I'M MAKING A CAKE!
WHA... WHY?
I LIKE CAKE!
WE'RE ON DUTY, YOU-HEY! WATCH OUT!
SPLOOSH!
OOPS. I MIGHT HAVE ADDED TOO MUCH CUSTARD POWDER...
WHEEEEE!
UNGH!
SPLOOSH!
PD
OW!
ARGH!
I AWARD OFFICER DIPLODOOFUS THE MEDAL OF SUPER BRAVERY FOR SINGLEHANDEDLY BUSTING TWO PERPS!
IT WAS A PIECE OF CAKE!
OH, DON'T BE SO MODEST
ISN'T THIS AMAZING, ART MONKEY?
MY MECHANICAL MARVEL WILL RENDER ALL COMICS ARTISTS COMPLETELY UNNECESSARY!
OOK.

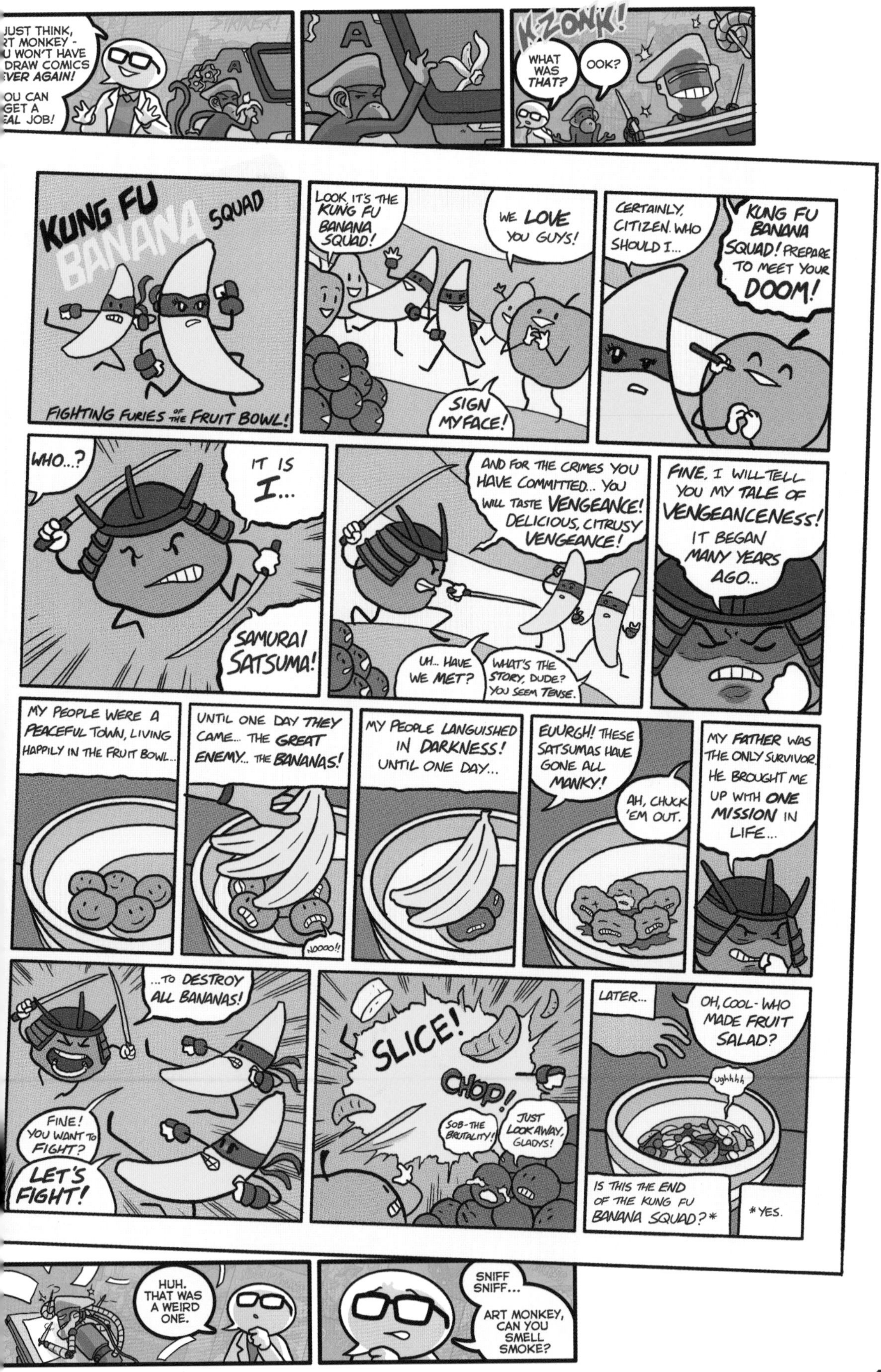

JUST THINK, RT MONKEY - U WON'T HAVE DRAW COMICS EVER AGAIN!
OU CAN GET A EAL JOB!
KZONK!
WHAT WAS THAT?
OOK?
KUNG FU BANANA SQUAD
FIGHTING FURIES OF THE FRUIT BOWL!
LOOK IT'S THE KUNG FU BANANA SQUAD!
WE LOVE YOU GUYS!
SIGN MY FACE!
CERTAINLY, CITIZEN. WHO SHOULD I...
KUNG FU BANANA SQUAD! PREPARE TO MEET YOUR DOOM!
WHO...?
IT IS I...
SAMURAI SATSUMA!
AND FOR THE CRIMES YOU HAVE COMMITTED... YOU WILL TASTE VENGEANCE! DELICIOUS, CITRUSY VENGEANCE!
UH... HAVE WE MET?
WHAT'S THE STORY, DUDE? YOU SEEM TENSE.
FINE. I WILL TELL YOU MY TALE OF VENGEANCENESS! IT BEGAN MANY YEARS AGO...
MY PEOPLE WERE A PEACEFUL TOWN, LIVING HAPPILY IN THE FRUIT BOWL...
UNTIL ONE DAY THEY CAME... THE GREAT ENEMY... THE BANANAS!
NOOOO!!
MY PEOPLE LANGUISHED IN DARKNESS! UNTIL ONE DAY...
EUURGH! THESE SATSUMAS HAVE GONE ALL MANKY!
AH, CHUCK 'EM OUT.
MY FATHER WAS THE ONLY SURVIVOR. HE BROUGHT ME UP WITH ONE MISSION IN LIFE...
...TO DESTROY ALL BANANAS!
FINE! YOU WANT TO FIGHT?
LET'S FIGHT!
SLICE!
CHOP!
SOB-THE BRUTALITY!
JUST LOOK AWAY, GLADYS!
LATER...
OH, COOL- WHO MADE FRUIT SALAD?
ughhhh
IS THIS THE END OF THE KUNG FU BANANA SQUAD?*
*YES.
HUH. THAT WAS A WEIRD ONE.
SNIFF SNIFF...
ART MONKEY, CAN YOU SMELL SMOKE?

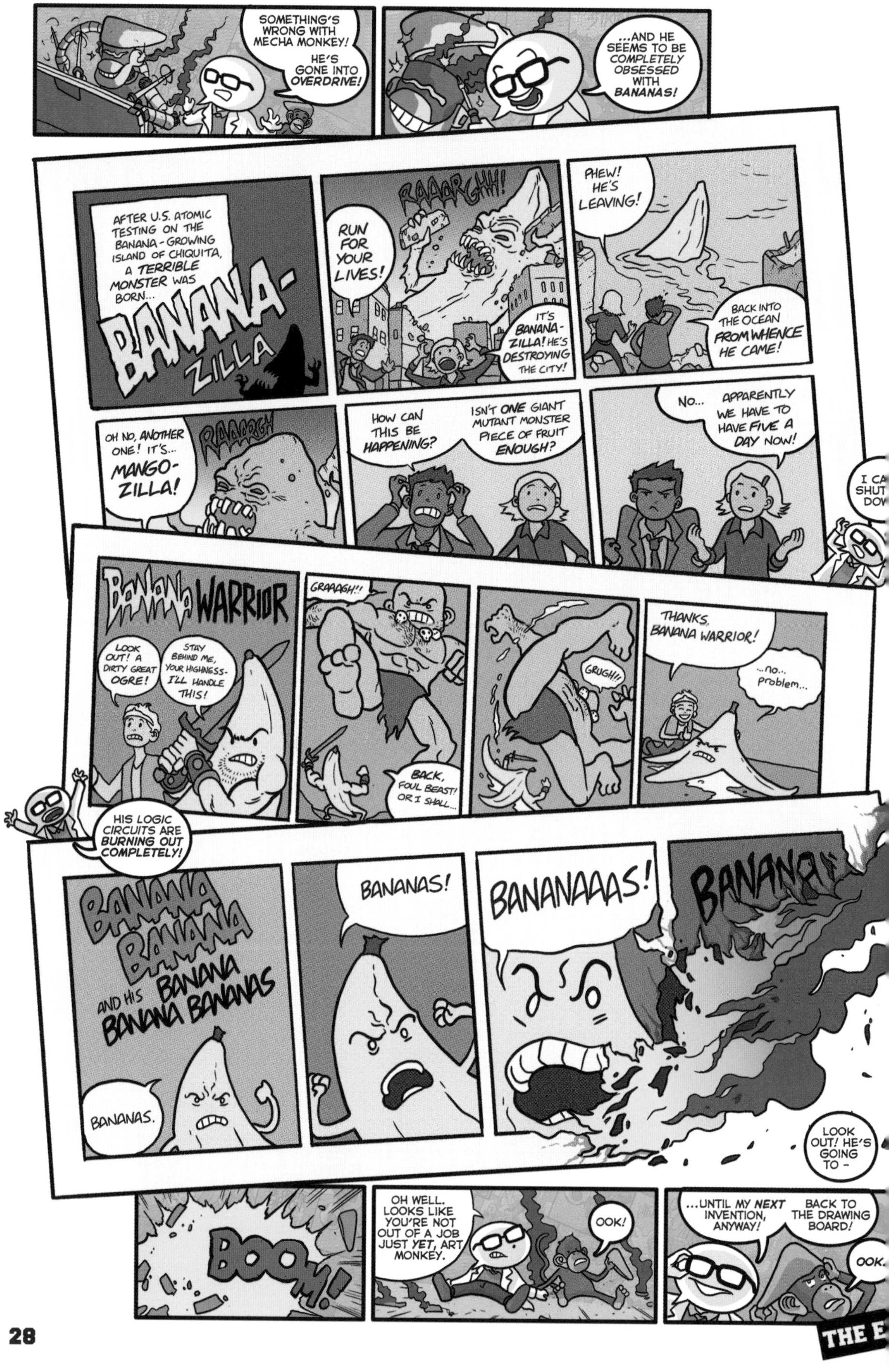
SOMETHING'S WRONG WITH MECHA MONKEY!
HE'S GONE INTO OVERDRIVE!
...AND HE SEEMS TO BE COMPLETELY OBSESSED WITH BANANAS!
AFTER U.S. ATOMIC TESTING ON THE BANANA-GROWING ISLAND OF CHIQUITA, A TERRIBLE MONSTER WAS BORN...
BANANA-ZILLA
RAAARGHH!
RUN FOR YOUR LIVES!
IT'S BANANA-ZILLA! HE'S DESTROYING THE CITY!
PHEW! HE'S LEAVING!
BACK INTO THE OCEAN FROM WHENCE HE CAME!
OH NO, ANOTHER ONE! IT'S... MANGO-ZILLA!
RAAARGH
HOW CAN THIS BE HAPPENING?
ISN'T ONE GIANT MUTANT MONSTER PIECE OF FRUIT ENOUGH?
NO... APPARENTLY WE HAVE TO HAVE FIVE A DAY NOW!
BANANA WARRIOR
LOOK OUT! A DIRTY GREAT OGRE!
STAY BEHIND ME, YOUR HIGHNESS- I'LL HANDLE THIS!
GRAAAGH!!
BACK, FOUL BEAST! OR I SHALL...
GRUGH!!
THANKS, BANANA WARRIOR!
...no... problem...
HIS LOGIC CIRCUITS ARE BURNING OUT COMPLETELY!
BANANA BANANA BANANA AND HIS BANANA BANANA BANANAS
BANANAS.
BANANAS!
BANANAAAS!
BANANA
LOOK OUT! HE'S GOING TO -
BOOM!
OH WELL. LOOKS LIKE YOU'RE NOT OUT OF A JOB JUST YET, ART MONKEY.
OOK!
...UNTIL MY NEXT INVENTION, ANYWAY!
BACK TO THE DRAWING BOARD!
OOK.
THE E

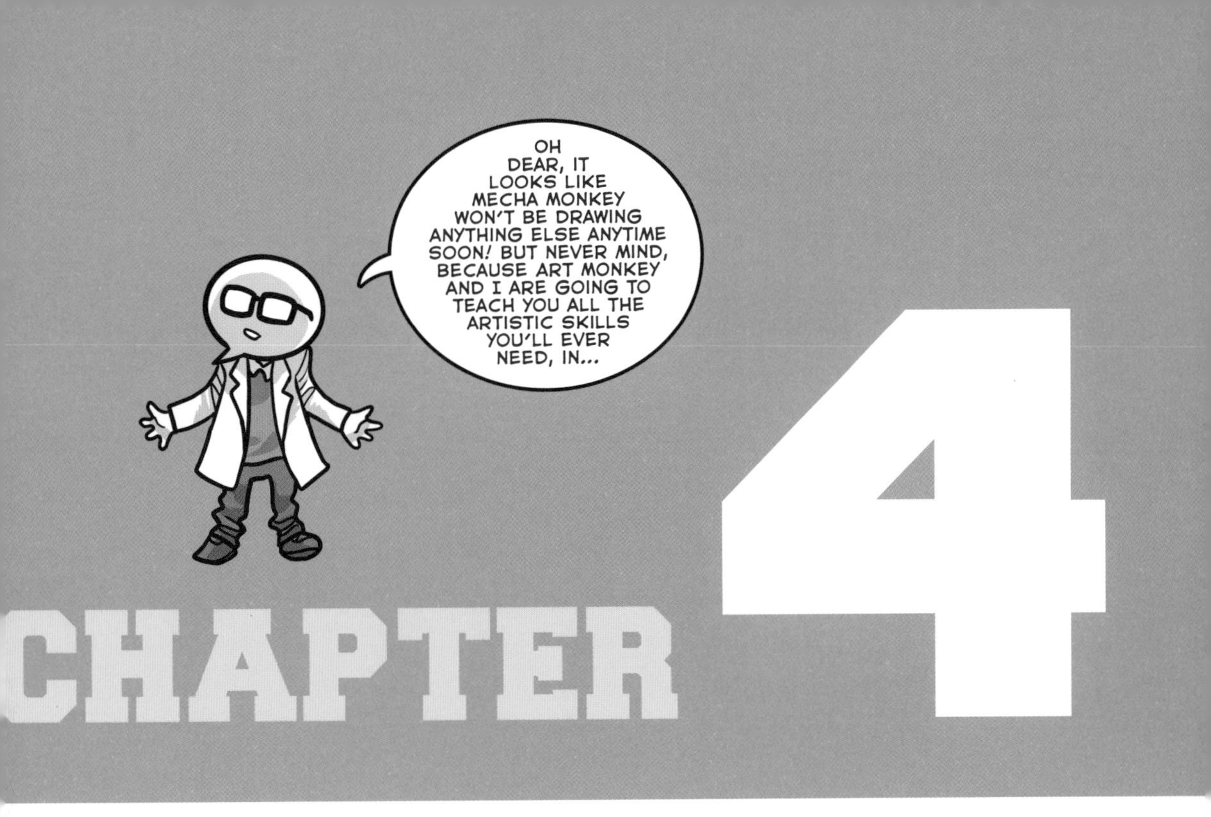
OH DEAR, IT LOOKS LIKE MECHA MONKEY WON'T BE DRAWING ANYTHING ELSE ANYTIME SOON! BUT NEVER MIND, BECAUSE ART MONKEY AND I ARE GOING TO TEACH YOU ALL THE ARTISTIC SKILLS YOU'LL EVER NEED, IN...

CHAPTER 4

HOW TO DRAW ANYTHING (AWESOMELY)

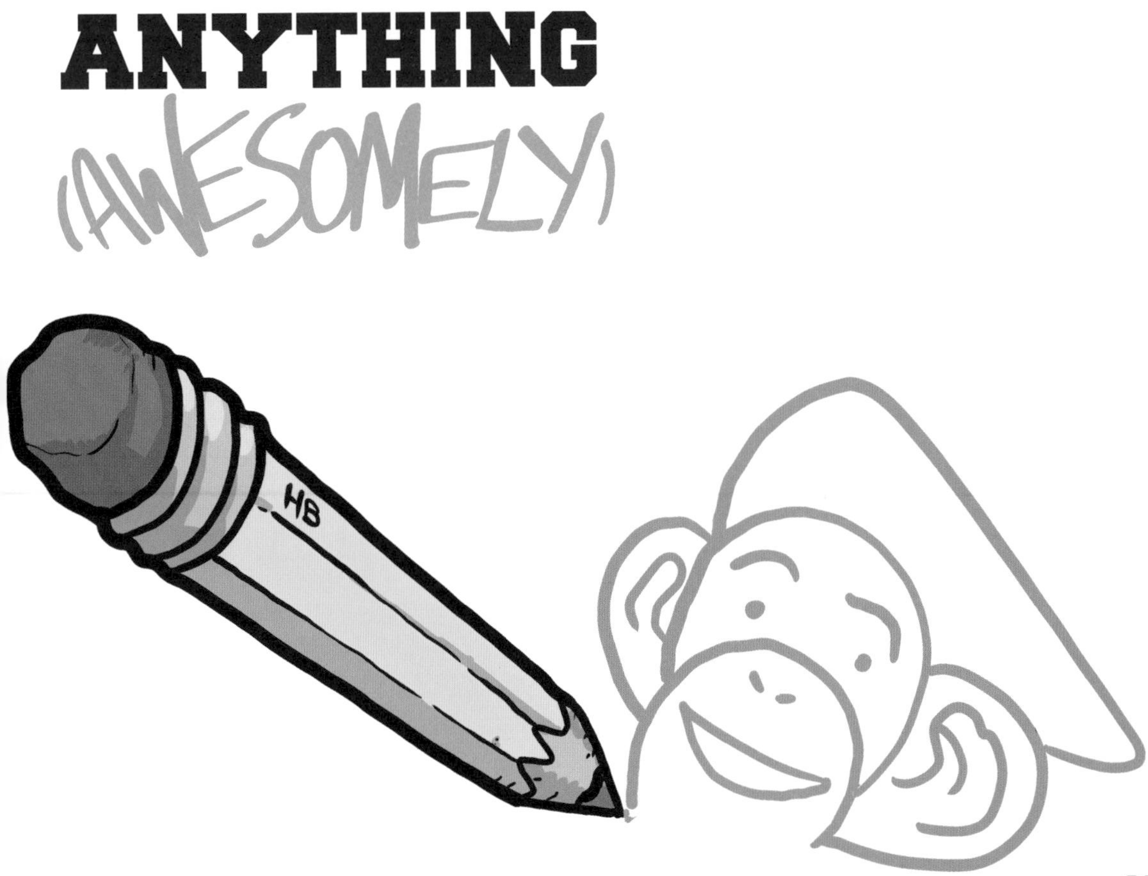
HB

HOW TO DRAW
ANYTHING*
(AWESOMELY)

*NO, REALLY!

AND NOW, WE'RE GOING TO TEACH YOU HOW TO DRAW ANYTHING!

VAMPIRES, NINJAS, MONSTERS, JELLYFISH... *ANYTHING!*

SEE, WHATEVER SORT OF CHARACTERS YOU'RE DRAWING, MOST ARE BASICALLY *PERSON* SHAPED.

AND *PERSON* SHAPES ARE *EASY* TO DRAW!

JUST DRAW A CIRCLE FOR THE HEAD...

AND THEN A BOX UNDERNEATH IT...

...LITTLE BOXES FOR THE ARMS AND LEGS...

THEN DRAW AROUND THEM IN PEN AND...

TA-D

THAT'S ALL THERE IS TO IT! YOU CAN MAKE YOUR CHARACTERS DO ANYTHING, WITH JUST THOSE SAME BASIC SHAPES!

RUNNING!

JUMPING!

SLIPPING ON A BANANA!

STUPID... PLACE... TO LEAVE A BANANA...

AND YOU CAN TURN THOSE SAME SHAPES INTO *ANYTHING!*

A *PIRATE!*

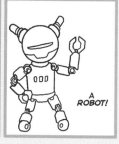

A *ROBOT!*

A *PRINCESS!*

A *JELLYFISH!*

UM...

OKAY, JELLYFIS ARE A B DIFFEREN

ART MONKEY CHALLENGE!

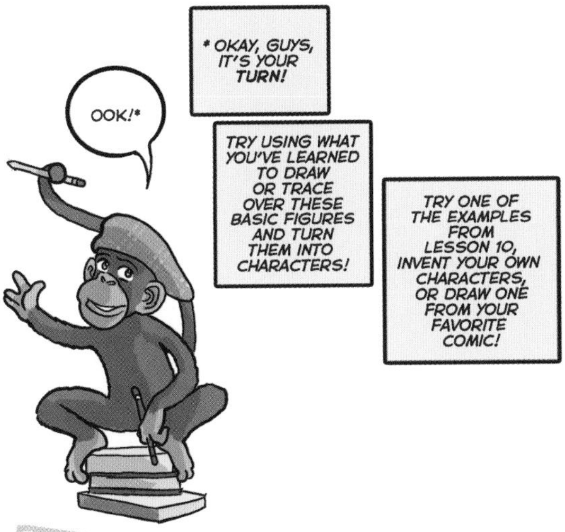

OOK!*
* OKAY, GUYS, IT'S YOUR TURN!
TRY USING WHAT YOU'VE LEARNED TO DRAW OR TRACE OVER THESE BASIC FIGURES AND TURN THEM INTO CHARACTERS!
TRY ONE OF THE EXAMPLES FROM LESSON 10, INVENT YOUR OWN CHARACTERS, OR DRAW ONE FROM YOUR FAVORITE COMIC!

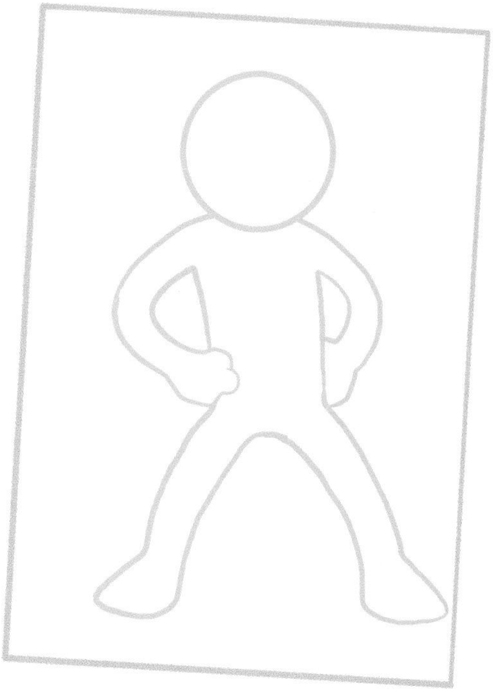

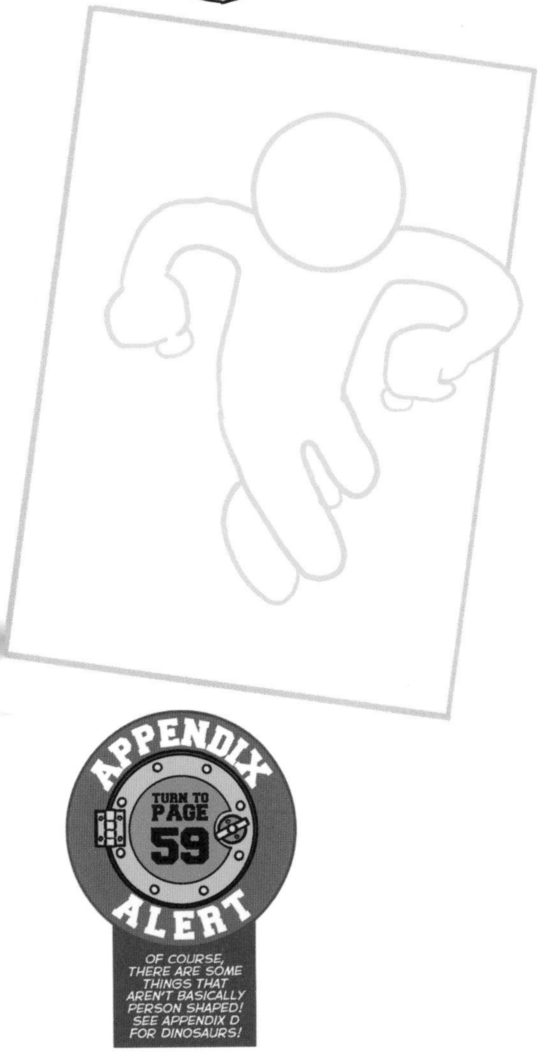

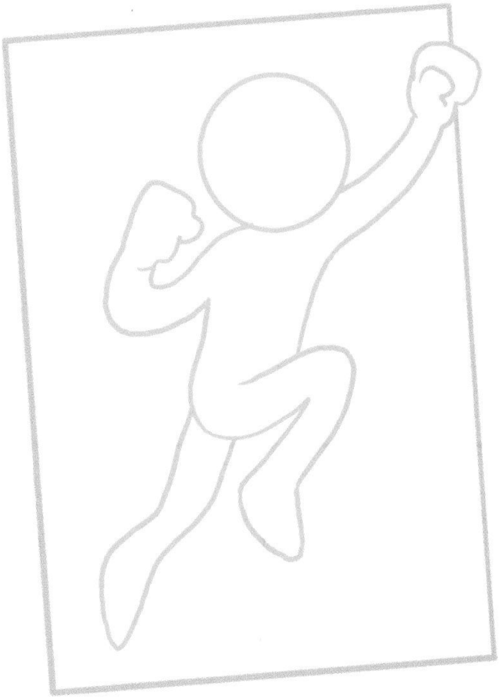

APPENDIX ALERT

TURN TO PAGE 59

OF COURSE, THERE ARE SOME THINGS THAT AREN'T BASICALLY PERSON SHAPED! SEE APPENDIX D FOR DINOSAURS!

LESSON 11: HOW TO DRAW CARTOONS (AWESOMELY)

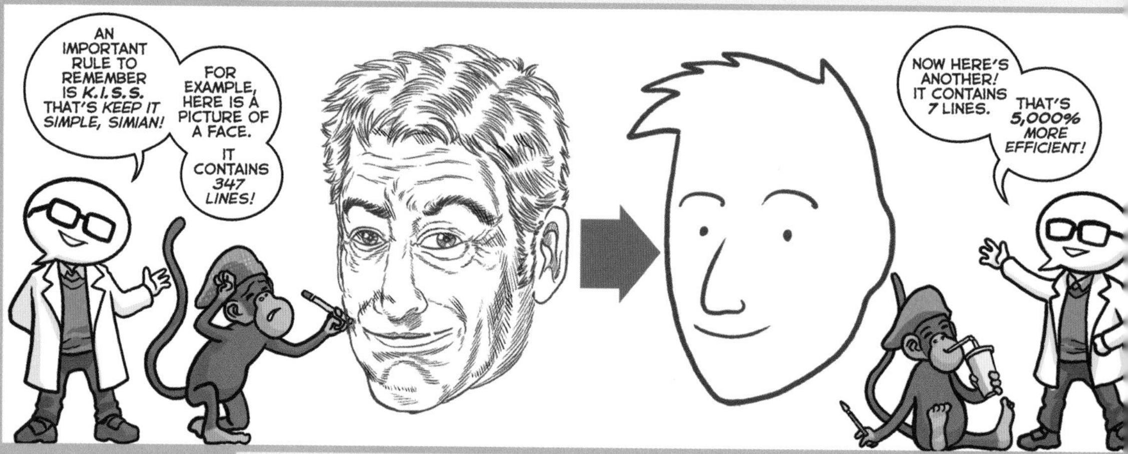
AN IMPORTANT RULE TO REMEMBER IS *K.I.S.S.* THAT'S *KEEP IT SIMPLE, SIMIAN!*
FOR EXAMPLE, HERE IS A PICTURE OF A FACE.
IT CONTAINS *347 LINES!*
NOW HERE'S ANOTHER! IT CONTAINS *7* LINES.
THAT'S *5,000% MORE EFFICIENT!*

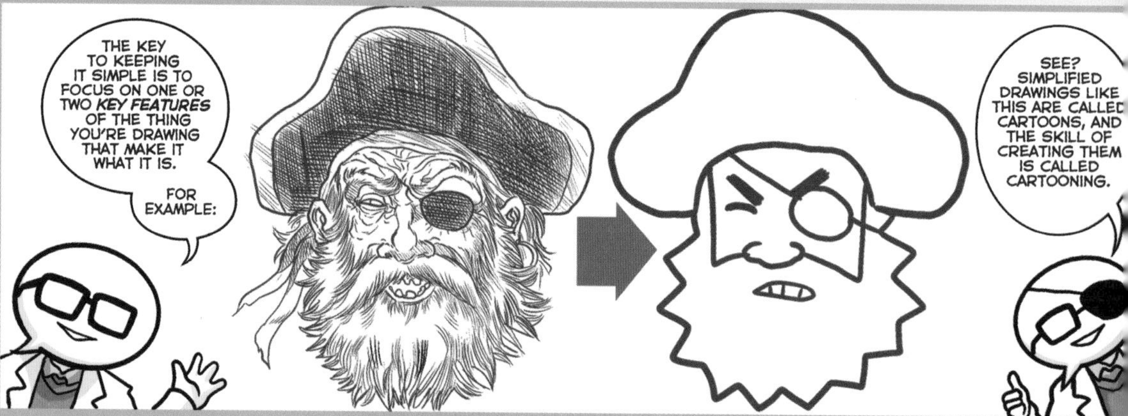
THE KEY TO KEEPING IT SIMPLE IS TO FOCUS ON ONE OR TWO *KEY FEATURES* OF THE THING YOU'RE DRAWING THAT MAKE IT WHAT IT IS.
FOR EXAMPLE:
SEE? SIMPLIFIED DRAWINGS LIKE THIS ARE CALLED CARTOONS, AND THE SKILL OF CREATING THEM IS CALLED CARTOONING.

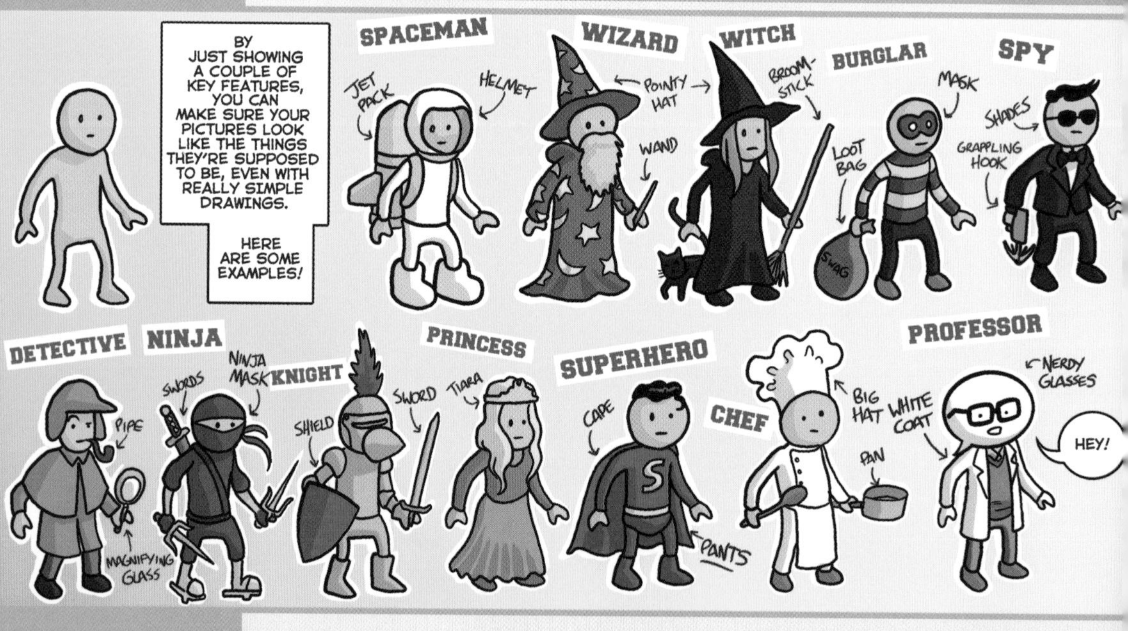
BY JUST SHOWING A COUPLE OF KEY FEATURES, YOU CAN MAKE SURE YOUR PICTURES LOOK LIKE THE THINGS THEY'RE SUPPOSED TO BE, EVEN WITH REALLY SIMPLE DRAWINGS.
HERE ARE SOME EXAMPLES!
SPACEMAN
JET PACK
HELMET
WIZARD
POINTY HAT
WAND
WITCH
BROOM-STICK
BURGLAR
MASK
LOOT BAG
SWAG
SPY
SHADES
GRAPPLING HOOK
DETECTIVE
PIPE
MAGNIFYING GLASS
NINJA
SWORDS
NINJA MASK
KNIGHT
SHIELD
SWORD
PRINCESS
TIARA
SUPERHERO
CAPE
PANTS
CHEF
BIG HAT
PAN
PROFESSOR
NERDY GLASSES
WHITE COAT
HEY!

ART MONKEY CHALLENGE!

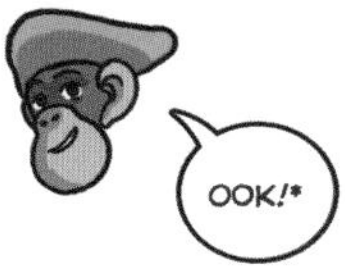
OOK!*

*HERE IS A **PIRATE ORANGUTAN!**

THIS IS A VERY DETAILED DRAWING. TRY DRAWING YOUR OWN **CARTOONIFIED** VERSION!

JUST THINK ABOUT WHAT HIS **KEY FEATURES** ARE, AND TRY DRAWING A SUPER-SIMPLE VERSION OF THEM!

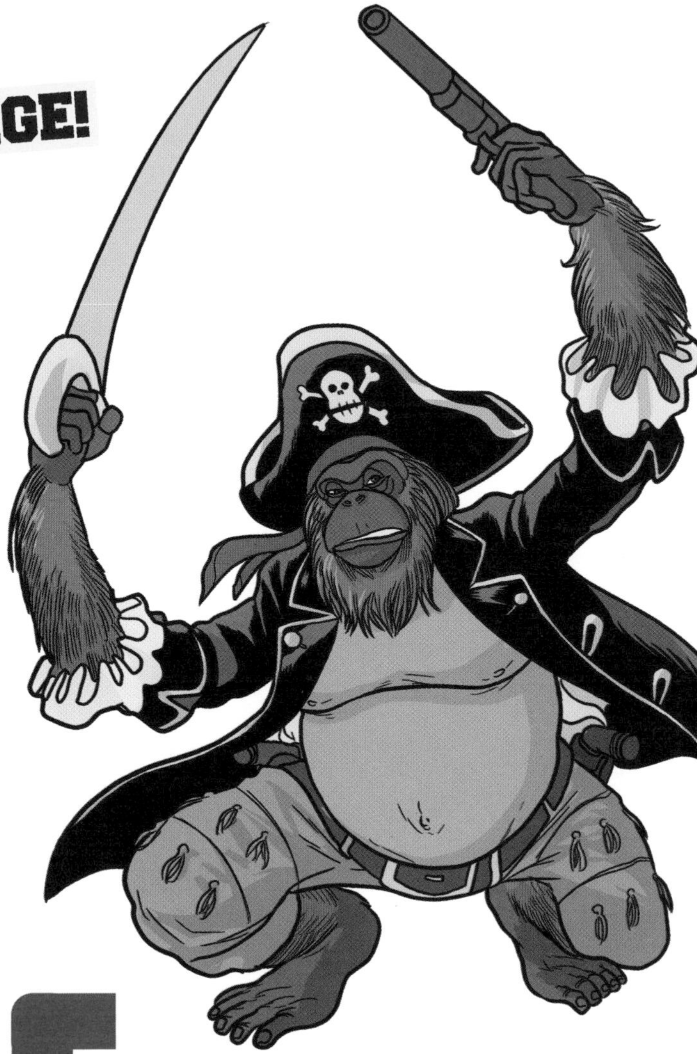

LESSON 12: HOW TO DRAW (AWESOME) FACES

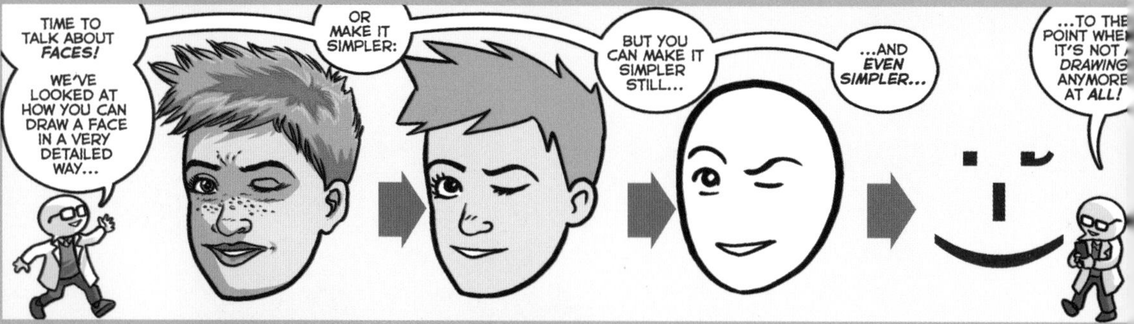

TIME TO TALK ABOUT *FACES!*
WE'VE LOOKED AT HOW YOU CAN DRAW A FACE IN A VERY DETAILED WAY...
OR MAKE IT SIMPLER:
BUT YOU CAN MAKE IT SIMPLER STILL...
...AND *EVEN SIMPLER...*
...TO THE POINT WHE IT'S NOT *DRAWING* ANYMORE AT *ALL!*

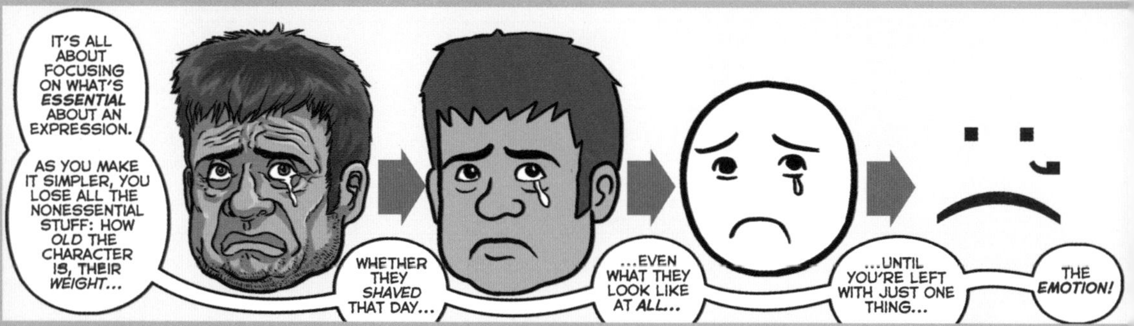

IT'S ALL ABOUT FOCUSING ON WHAT'S *ESSENTIAL* ABOUT AN EXPRESSION.
AS YOU MAKE IT SIMPLER, YOU LOSE ALL THE NONESSENTIAL STUFF: HOW *OLD* THE CHARACTER IS, THEIR *WEIGHT...*
WHETHER THEY *SHAVED* THAT DAY...
...EVEN WHAT THEY LOOK LIKE AT *ALL...*
...UNTIL YOU'RE LEFT WITH JUST ONE THING...
THE *EMOTION!*

FOCUS ON WHAT'S HAPPENING IN ***THREE KEY AREAS:***

- THE ***EYES***
- THE ***EYEBROWS***
- THE ***MOUTH***

AND YOU CAN USE REALLY SIMPLE DRAWINGS TO SHOW A WHOLE ***RANGE*** OF EMOTIONS...

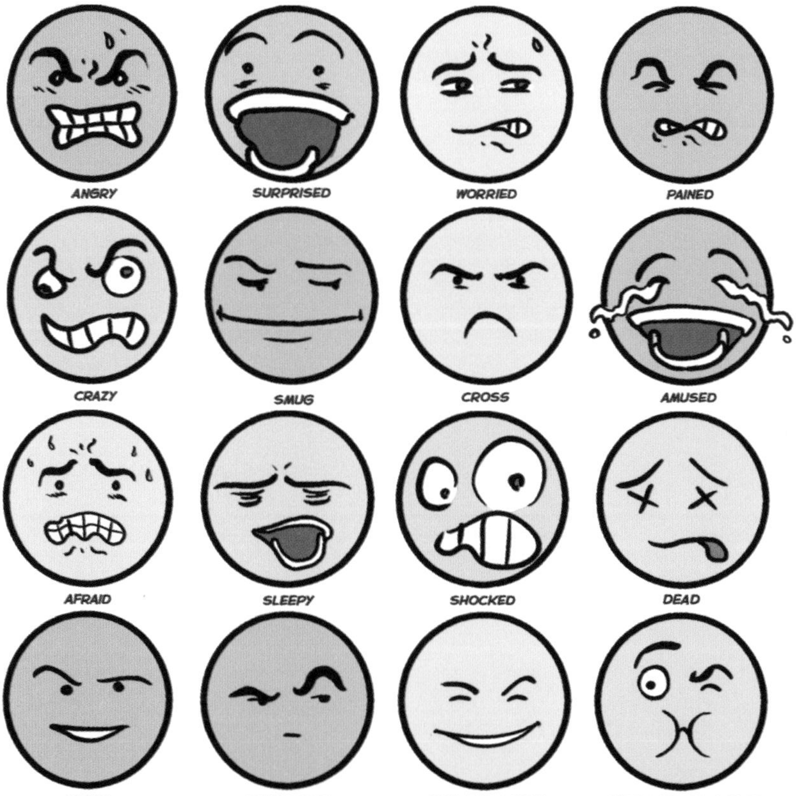

ANGRY
SURPRISED
WORRIED
PAINED
CRAZY
SMUG
CROSS
AMUSED
AFRAID
SLEEPY
SHOCKED
DEAD
COCKY
SUSPICIOUS
JUST LAID A FART
JUST SMELLED A FART

ART MONKEY CHALLENGE!

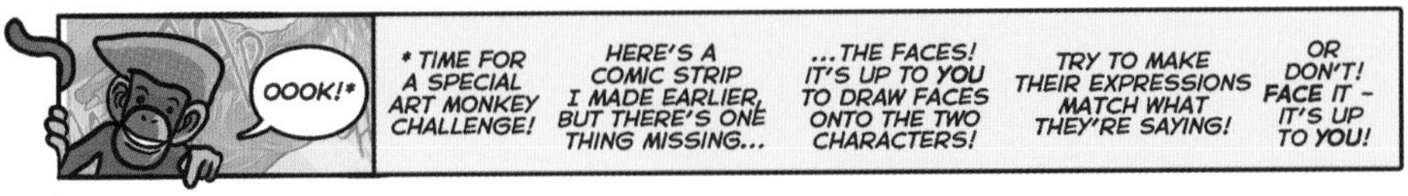
OOOK!*
* TIME FOR A SPECIAL ART MONKEY CHALLENGE!
HERE'S A COMIC STRIP I MADE EARLIER, BUT THERE'S ONE THING MISSING...
...THE FACES! IT'S UP TO YOU TO DRAW FACES ONTO THE TWO CHARACTERS!
TRY TO MAKE THEIR EXPRESSIONS MATCH WHAT THEY'RE SAYING!
OR DON'T! FACE IT - IT'S UP TO YOU!

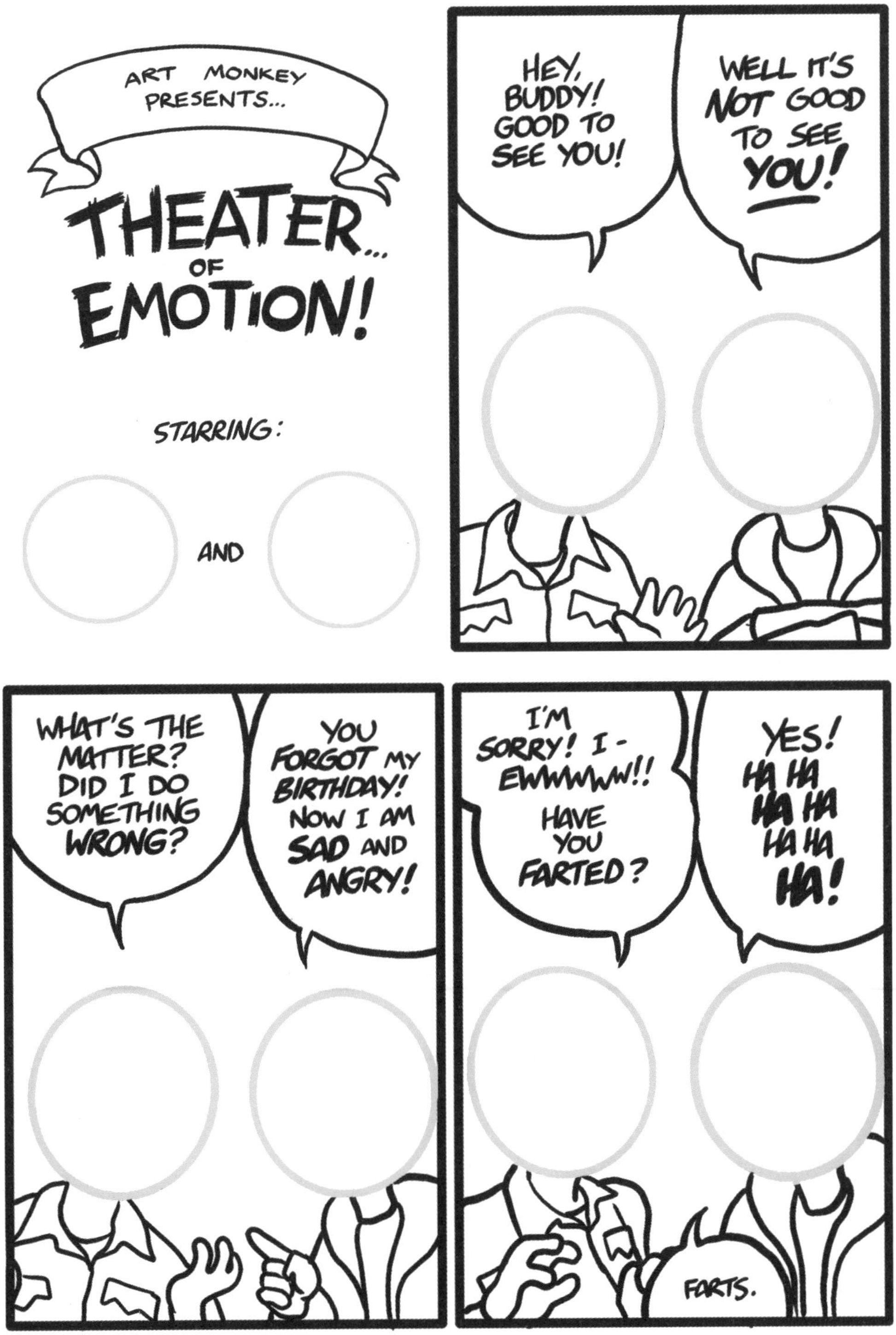
ART MONKEY PRESENTS...
THEATER... OF EMOTION!
STARRING:
AND
HEY, BUDDY! GOOD TO SEE YOU!
WELL IT'S NOT GOOD TO SEE YOU!
WHAT'S THE MATTER? DID I DO SOMETHING WRONG?
YOU FORGOT MY BIRTHDAY! NOW I AM SAD AND ANGRY!
I'M SORRY! I - EWWWWW!! HAVE YOU FARTED?
YES! HA HA HA HA HA HA HA!
FARTS.

LESSON 13: HOW TO DRAW (AWESOME) ROBOTS

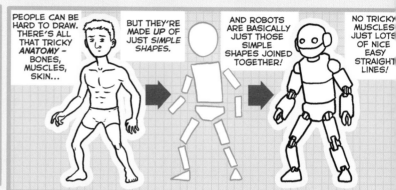

ROBOTS! NOT ONLY ARE ROBOTS ONE OF THE **MOST AWESOMEST THINGS OF ALL**, THEY ARE ALSO SUPER EASY TO DRAW!

LET'S SEE!

PEOPLE CAN BE HARD TO DRAW. THERE'S ALL THAT TRICKY **ANATOMY** – BONES, MUSCLES, SKIN...

BUT THEY'RE MADE **UP** OF JUST **SIMPLE** SHAPES.

AND ROBOTS ARE BASICALLY JUST THOSE SIMPLE SHAPES JOINED TOGETHER!

NO TRICKY MUSCLES, JUST LOTS OF NICE EASY STRAIGHT LINES!

ROBOTS AREN'T JUST HUMAN, EITHER! YOU CAN TURN ANYTHING INTO SIMPLE SHAPES.

JUST FIND THE MOST **BASIC SHAPES** THAT MAKE SOMETHING UP...

THOSE SAME SHAPES WILL JOIN TOGETHER TO CREATE A **ROBOT**!

(...MAYBE ADD SOME **MISSILES**, FOR GOOD LUCK!)

(**EVERYONE** LOVES MISSILES!)

THE TRICK TO MAKING YOUR ROBOT LOOK AMAZING IS TO THINK ABOUT HOW THE SIMPLE SHAPES **JOIN TOGETHER**! THE DETAIL YOU PUT IN THE **JOINTS** WILL REALLY BRING YOUR ROBOT TO LIFE!

HINGED JOINTS (ELBOWS, KNEES) – MOVE IN ONE DIRECTION!

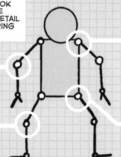

BALL + SOCKET JOINTS (E.G. SHOULDERS, HIPS) – MOVE IN ALL DIRECTIONS.

OR, HEY, THEY'RE **ROBOTS** – PUT SOME CRAZY ROBOT PIPES ON THERE!

APPENDIX ALERT

TURN TO PAGE **58**

HAVE A LOOK AT APPENDIX B FOR LOADS OF COOL ACCESSORIES TO ADD TO YOUR ROBOTS!

EASY, RIGHT? JUST SIMPLE SHAPES WITH DETAILED JOINTS! (AND SOME MISSILES)

ONCE YOU'VE GOT THE HANG OF THOSE BASICS, YOU CAN DRAW **ALL** DIFFERENT STYLES AND FLAVORS OF ROBOT!

MANGA

RETRO

RUSTY

ART MONKEY CHALLENGE!

OOK!*

* TIME TO PUT THOSE ROBOT-DRAWING SKILLS INTO **ACTION!**

HERE'S A THRILLING ROBOTIC COMIC STRIP FOR YOU TO FINISH OFF!

USE THE BASIC SHAPES BELOW TO INVENT YOUR OWN ROBOT! THINK ABOUT THE JOINTS, DETAILS, AND ACCESSORIES, AND WHAT STYLE IT WILL BE IN!

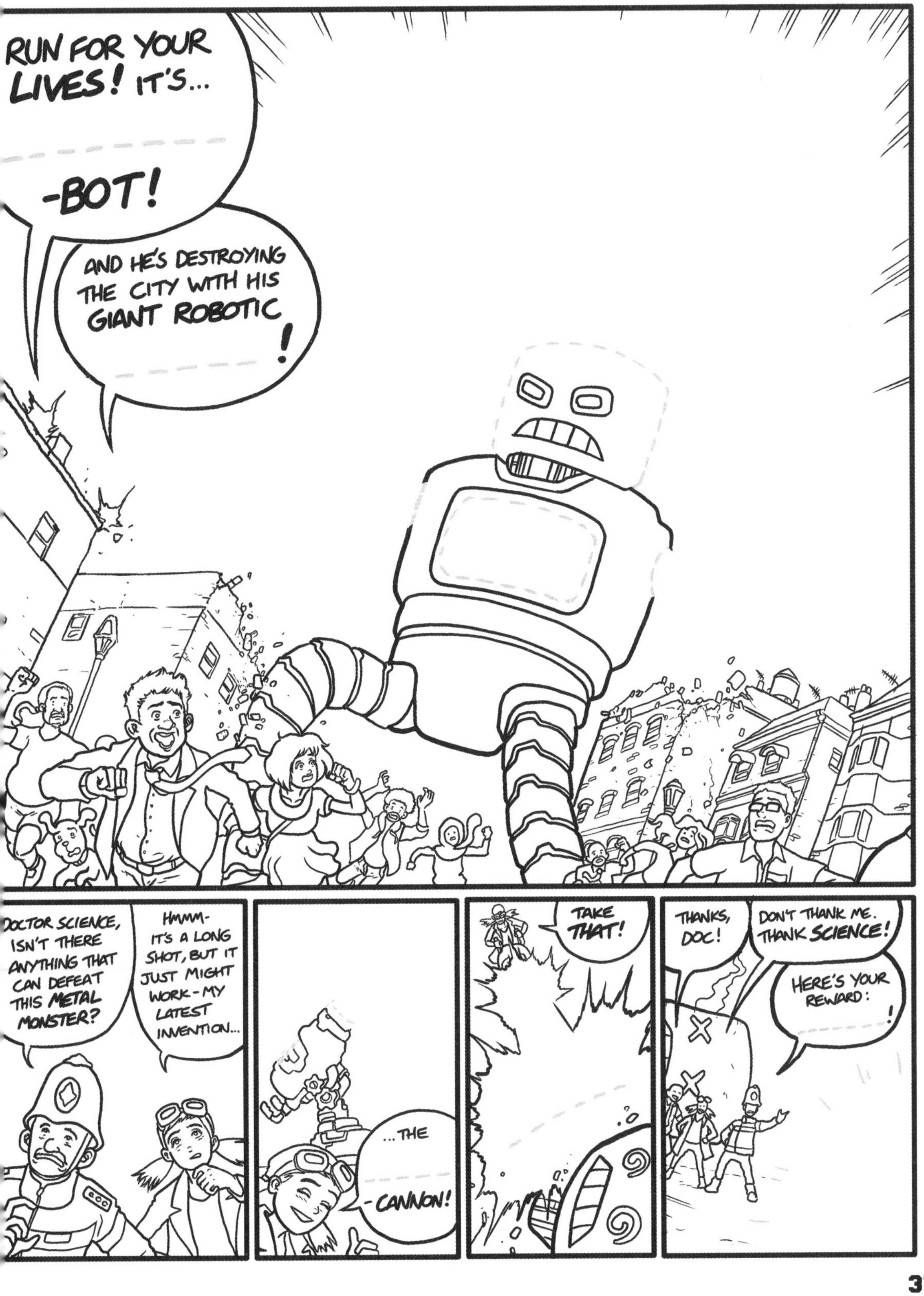
RUN FOR YOUR LIVES! IT'S...
-BOT!
AND HE'S DESTROYING THE CITY WITH HIS GIANT ROBOTIC
!
DOCTOR SCIENCE, ISN'T THERE ANYTHING THAT CAN DEFEAT THIS METAL MONSTER?
HMMM- IT'S A LONG SHOT, BUT IT JUST MIGHT WORK-MY LATEST INVENTION...
...THE
-CANNON!
TAKE THAT!
THANKS, DOC!
DON'T THANK ME. THANK SCIENCE!
HERE'S YOUR REWARD:
!

HOW TO DRAW (AWESOME) PIRATES

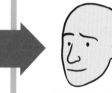

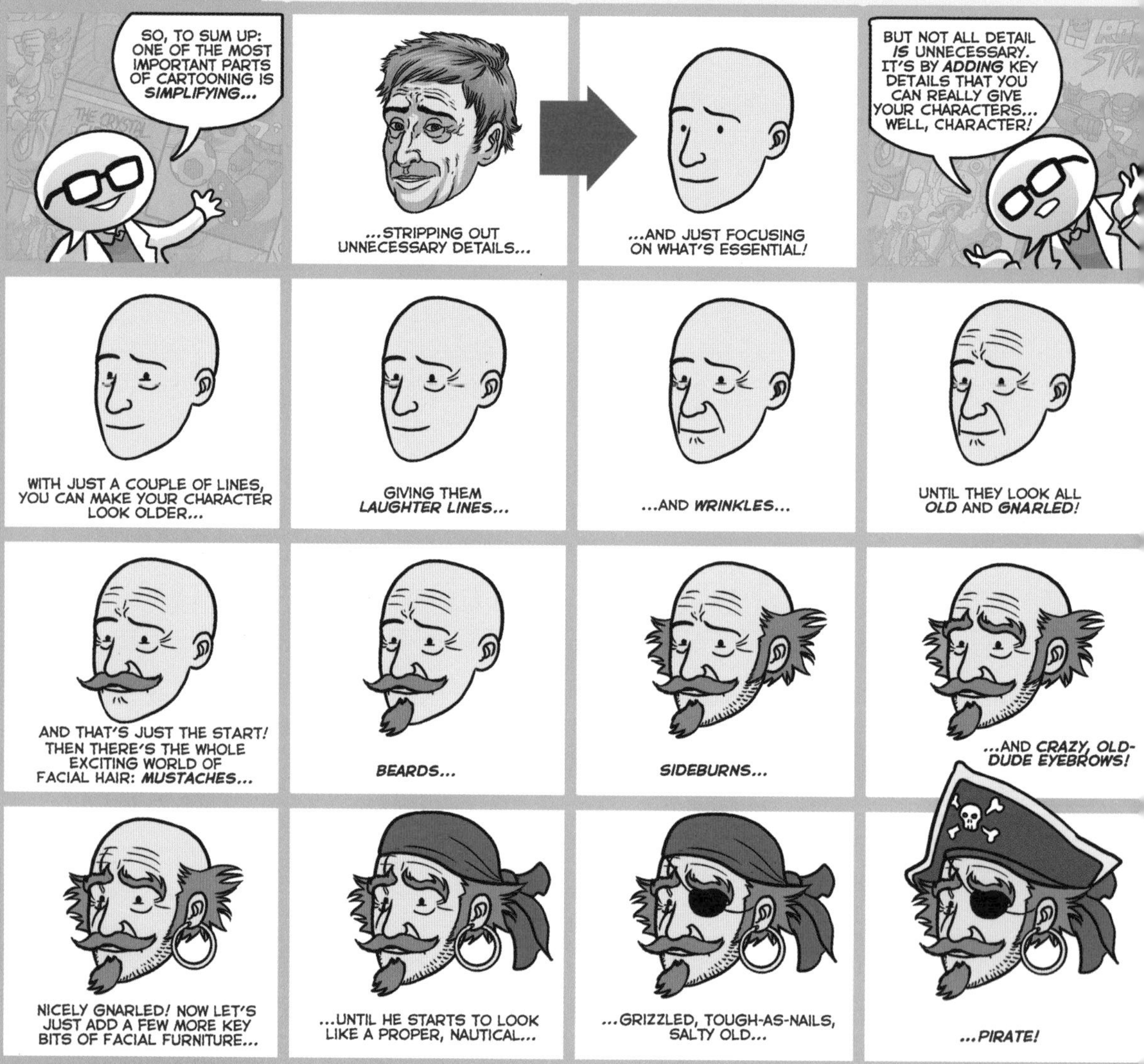

SO, TO SUM UP: ONE OF THE MOST IMPORTANT PARTS OF CARTOONING IS *SIMPLIFYING*...

...STRIPPING OUT UNNECESSARY DETAILS...

...AND JUST FOCUSING ON WHAT'S ESSENTIAL!

BUT NOT ALL DETAIL *IS* UNNECESSARY. IT'S BY *ADDING* KEY DETAILS THAT YOU CAN REALLY GIVE YOUR CHARACTERS... WELL, CHARACTER!

WITH JUST A COUPLE OF LINES, YOU CAN MAKE YOUR CHARACTER LOOK OLDER...

GIVING THEM *LAUGHTER LINES*...

...AND *WRINKLES*...

UNTIL THEY LOOK ALL *OLD* AND *GNARLED!*

AND THAT'S JUST THE START! THEN THERE'S THE WHOLE EXCITING WORLD OF FACIAL HAIR: *MUSTACHES*...

BEARDS...

SIDEBURNS...

...AND *CRAZY, OLD-DUDE EYEBROWS!*

NICELY GNARLED! NOW LET'S JUST ADD A FEW MORE KEY BITS OF FACIAL FURNITURE...

...UNTIL HE STARTS TO LOOK LIKE A PROPER, NAUTICAL...

...GRIZZLED, TOUGH-AS-NAILS, SALTY OLD...

...*PIRATE!*

ART MONKEY CHALLENGE!

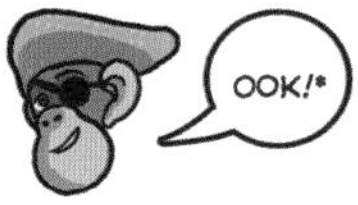
OOK!*

* HERE IS A NICE, FRIENDLY-LOOKING FELLOW!

...NOW SEE HOW MESSED-UP, GNARLY, AND PROPERLY PIRATEY YOU CAN MAKE HIM!

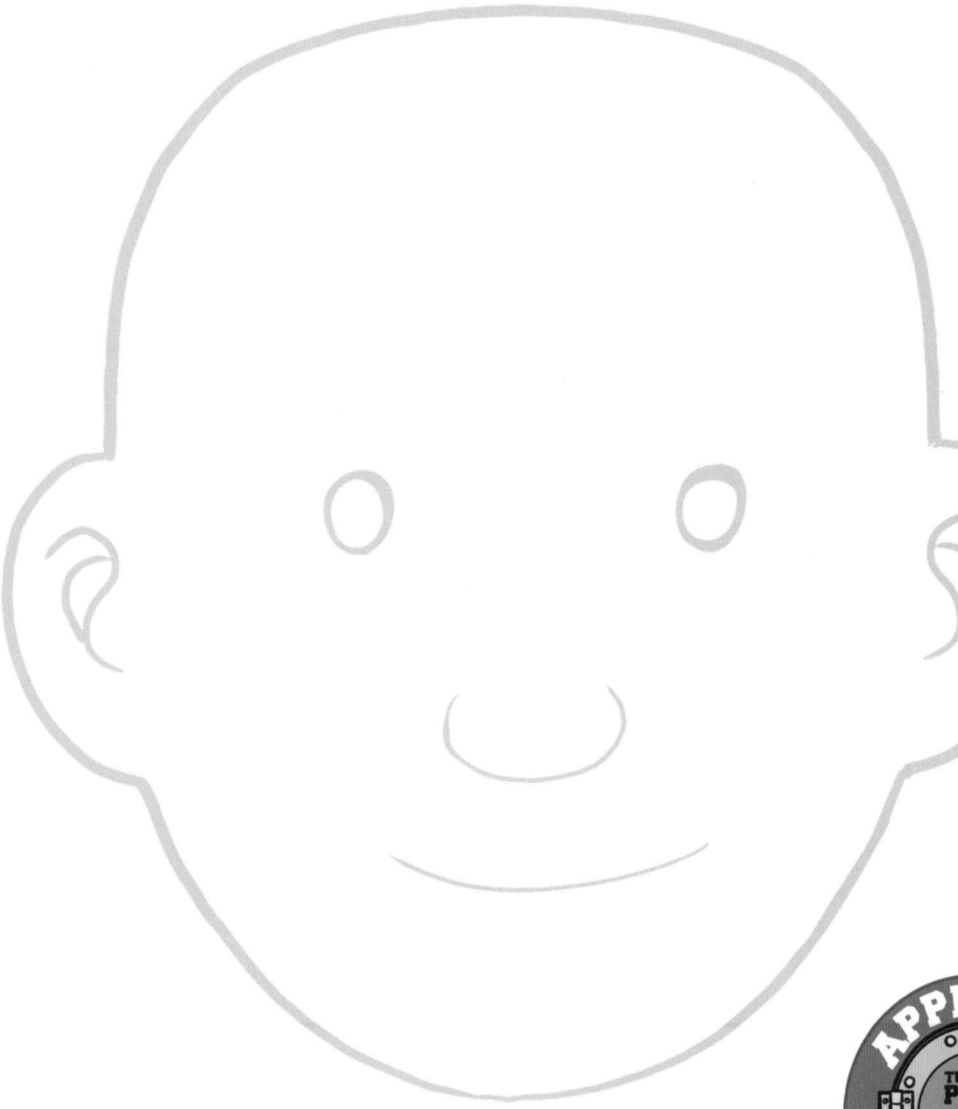

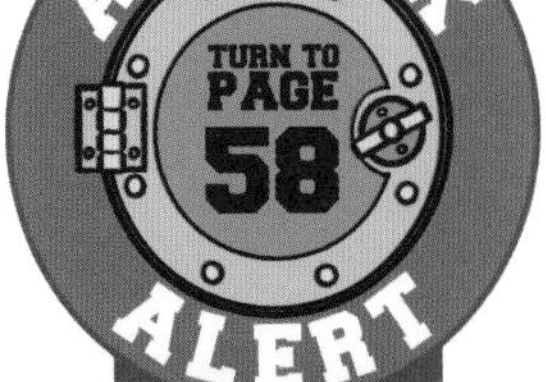
APPENDIX
TURN TO PAGE 58
ALERT

NEED SOME MORE INSPIRATION? CHECK OUT APPENDIX C FOR PIRATEY FACIAL HAIR!

HOW TO DRAW (AWESOME) MONSTERS

Panel 1:

REMEMBER MY PATENTED *AWESOMENESS PRINCIPLE* FROM CHAPTER 2? WELL, OF COURSE YOU DO. IT'S *AWESOME.*

THING THAT IS AWESOME + THING THAT IS AWESOME = **THING THAT IS TOTALLY SUPER AWESOME**

e.g. wizard + bear = **WIZARD BEAR**

Panel 2:

NOW, YOU MAY THINK THIS IS A NEW IDEA, BUT IN FACT IT'S SOMETHING THAT HUMANS HAVE BEEN USING SINCE...

...WELL, PRETTY MUCH SINCE THERE HAVE *BEEN* HUMANS!

Panel 3:

EVER SINCE THE *DAWN OF TIME,* PEOPLE HAVE BEEN PUTTING TWO THINGS TOGETHER TO MAKE SOMETHING NEW...

Panel 4 (large):

...AND COMING UP WITH ALL *MANNER* OF FREAKY AND FANTASTICAL CREATURES!

BONUS GAME! CAN YOU NAME ALL THE MONSTERS IN THIS PICTURE?

Panel 5:

TO MAKE YOUR MONSTERS LOOK COOL, TRY TAKING THE COOLEST OR THE *SCARIEST* PARTS OF DIFFERENT CREATURES...

CLAWS · TEETH · TENTACLES · TAILS · WINGS · LEGS · TUSKS · EYEBALLS · ANTENNAE

Panel 6:

...AND MIXING THEM UP TO MAKE SOMETHING *NEW!*

Panel 7:

...LIKE SO! YIKES!

Bottom section:

 OOK!*

* MIX AND MATCH THE PARTS OF THESE ANIMALS TO MAKE A MONSTER! GIVE IT AN *AWESOME MONSTER NAME!* DRAW YOUR FAVORITE ANIMAL IN THE BLANK SPACE TO ADD TO THE MIX!

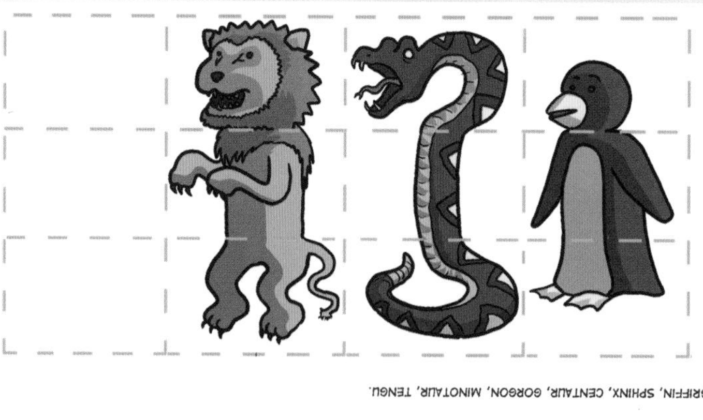

APPENDIX TURN TO PAGE **64** ALERT

ONCE YOU'VE MADE UP YOUR MONSTER, WHY NOT DRAW IT ON THE BONUS PIN-UP IN APPENDIX H?

BONUS GAME ANSWERS! GRIFFIN, SPHINX, CENTAUR, GORGON, MINOTAUR, TENGU.

SO, BY NOW YOU'VE GOT YOUR AWESOME IDEAS, AND YOU'RE READY TO START DRAWING THEM! BUT HOW DO YOU TURN THEM INTO ACTUAL STORIES? I'M GOING TO SHOW YOU SOME EASY WAYS TO DO JUST THAT! IT'S TIME FOR...

CHAPTER 5

HOW TO TELL (AWESOME) STORIES

LESSON 16: HOW TO TELL (AWESOME) STORIES

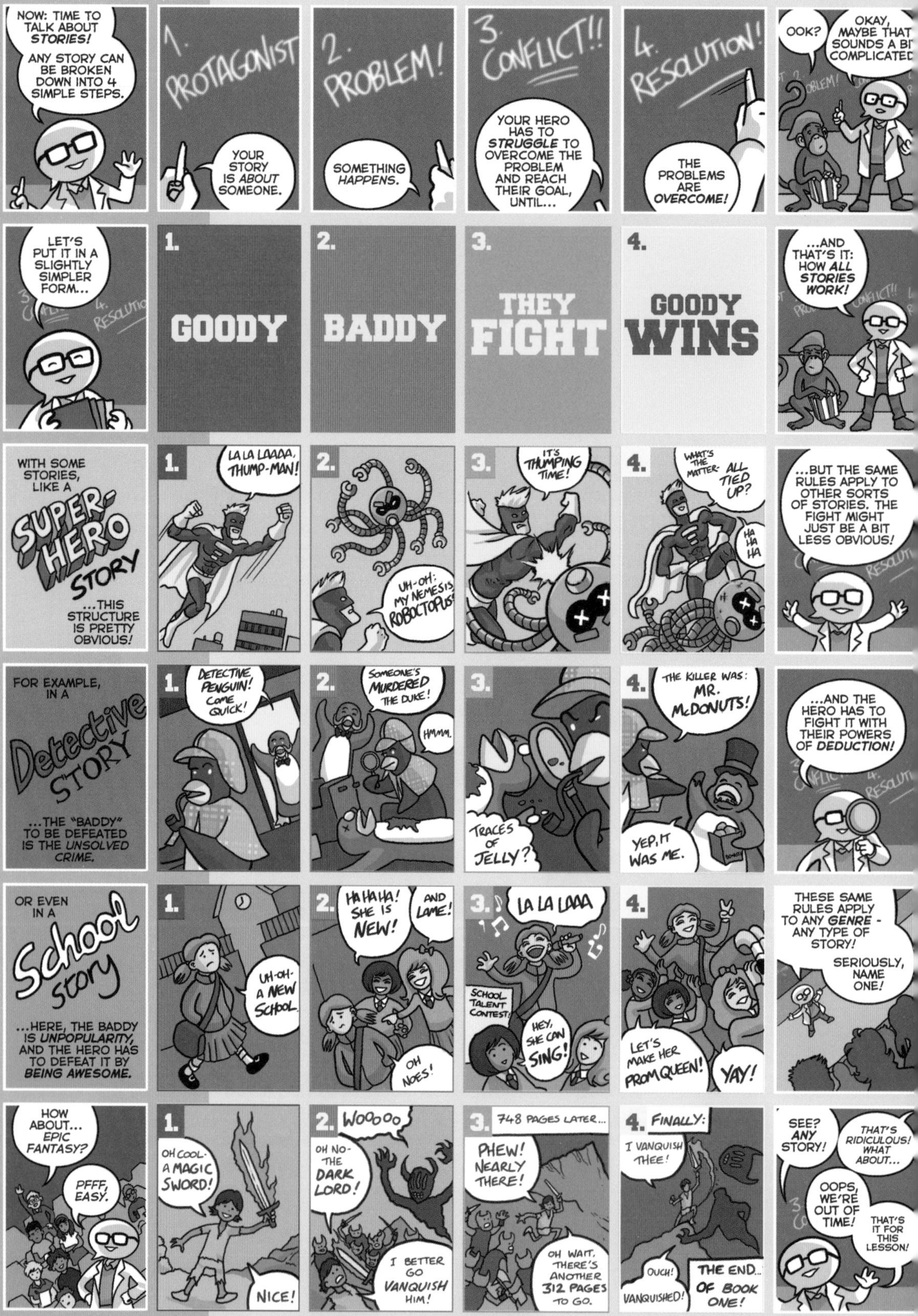

NOW: TIME TO TALK ABOUT STORIES!
ANY STORY CAN BE BROKEN DOWN INTO 4 SIMPLE STEPS.
1. PROTAGONIST
YOUR STORY IS ABOUT SOMEONE.
2. PROBLEM!
SOMETHING HAPPENS.
3. CONFLICT!!
YOUR HERO HAS TO STRUGGLE TO OVERCOME THE PROBLEM AND REACH THEIR GOAL, UNTIL...
4. RESOLUTION!
THE PROBLEMS ARE OVERCOME!
OOK?
OKAY, MAYBE THAT SOUNDS A BIT COMPLICATED
LET'S PUT IT IN A SLIGHTLY SIMPLER FORM...
1. GOODY
2. BADDY
3. THEY FIGHT
4. GOODY WINS
...AND THAT'S IT: HOW ALL STORIES WORK!
WITH SOME STORIES, LIKE A SUPER-HERO STORY ...THIS STRUCTURE IS PRETTY OBVIOUS!
1.
LA LA LAAAA, THUMP-MAN!
2.
UH-OH: MY NEMESIS, ROBOCTOPUS!
3.
IT'S THUMPING TIME!
4.
WHAT'S THE MATTER- ALL TIED UP?
HA HA HA
...BUT THE SAME RULES APPLY TO OTHER SORTS OF STORIES. THE FIGHT MIGHT JUST BE A BIT LESS OBVIOUS!
FOR EXAMPLE, IN A Detective STORY ...THE "BADDY" TO BE DEFEATED IS THE UNSOLVED CRIME.
1.
DETECTIVE PENGUIN! COME QUICK!
2.
SOMEONE'S MURDERED THE DUKE!
HMMM.
3.
TRACES OF JELLY?
4.
THE KILLER WAS: MR. McDONUTS!
YEP, IT WAS ME.
...AND THE HERO HAS TO FIGHT IT WITH THEIR POWERS OF DEDUCTION!
OR EVEN IN A School story ...HERE, THE BADDY IS UNPOPULARITY, AND THE HERO HAS TO DEFEAT IT BY BEING AWESOME.
1.
UH-OH- A NEW SCHOOL
2.
HA HA HA! SHE IS NEW!
AND LAME!
OH NOES!
3.
LA LA LAAA
SCHOOL TALENT CONTEST
HEY, SHE CAN SING!
4.
LET'S MAKE HER PROM QUEEN!
YAY!
THESE SAME RULES APPLY TO ANY GENRE - ANY TYPE OF STORY!
SERIOUSLY, NAME ONE!
HOW ABOUT... EPIC FANTASY?
PFFF, EASY.
1.
OH COOL- A MAGIC SWORD!
NICE!
2. WOOOOO
OH NO- THE DARK LORD!
I BETTER GO VANQUISH HIM!
3. 748 PAGES LATER...
PHEW! NEARLY THERE!
OH WAIT, THERE'S ANOTHER 312 PAGES TO GO.
4. FINALLY:
I VANQUISH THEE!
OUCH!
VANQUISHED!
THE END... OF BOOK ONE!
SEE? ANY STORY!
THAT'S RIDICULOUS! WHAT ABOUT...
OOPS, WE'RE OUT OF TIME!
THAT'S IT FOR THIS LESSON!

ART MONKEY CHALLENGE!

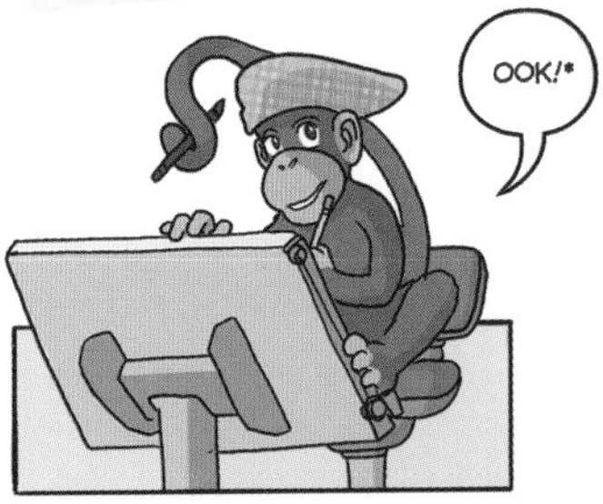
OOK!*

* DON'T WORRY, GUYS – THE PROF IS JUST WINDING YOU UP. HE KNOWS THERE ARE LOTS OF DIFFERENT WAYS TO TELL STORIES, REALLY!

...AT LEAST, I **THINK** HE DOES!

ANYWAY, IT'S TIME TO **TRY IT YOURSELF** – CHOOSE ONE OF YOUR OWN FAVORITE STORIES – IT COULD BE A BOOK, A FILM, OR ONE OF THE STORIES IN THIS VERY COMIC – AND TRY CONDENSING THE STORY INTO A FOUR-PANEL COMIC VERSION!

1. GOODY

2. BADDY

3. THEY FIGHT

4. GOODY WINS

LESSON 17: HOW TO CREATE (AWESOME) HEROES

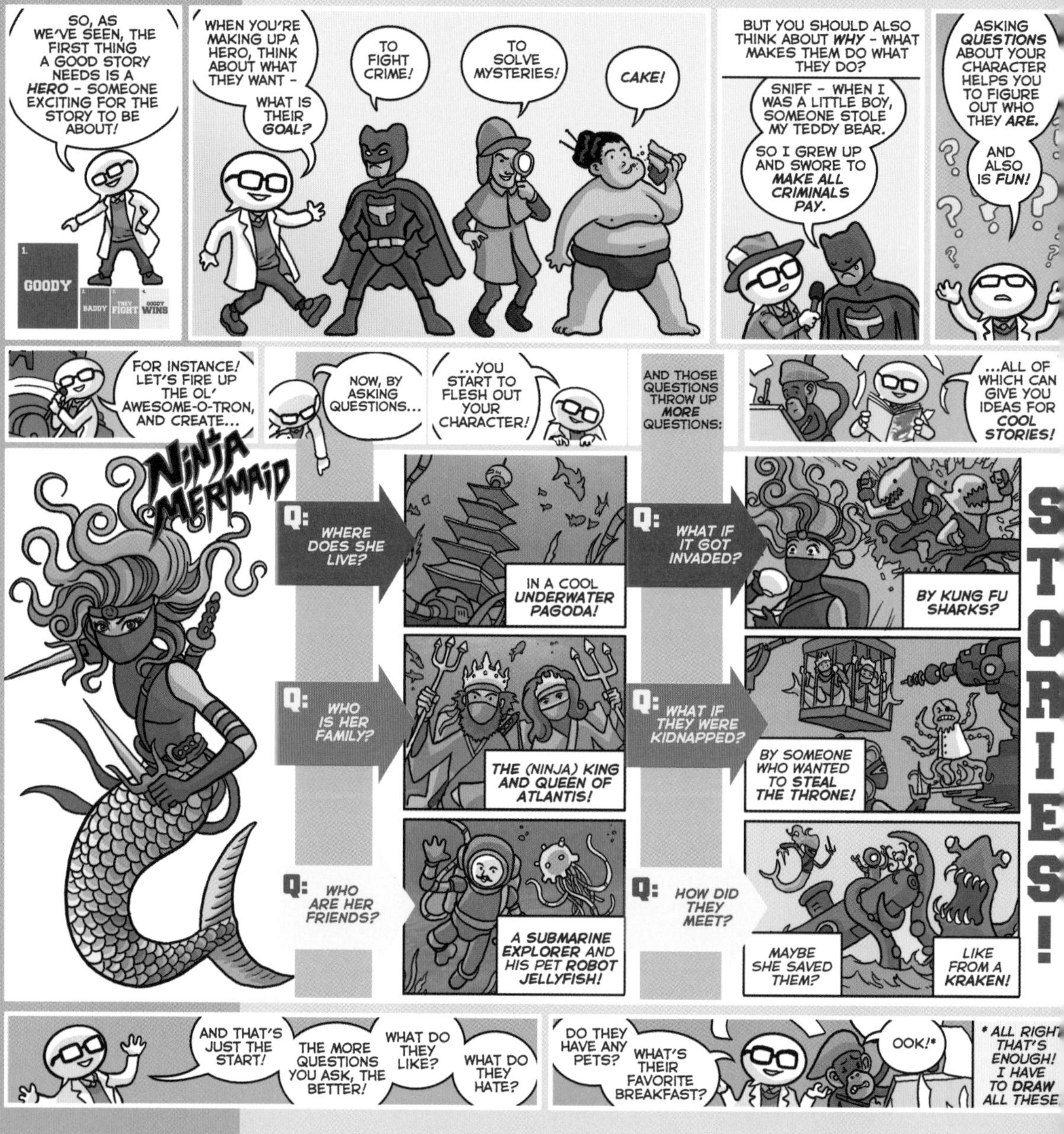

SO, AS WE'VE SEEN, THE FIRST THING A GOOD STORY NEEDS IS A HERO - SOMEONE EXCITING FOR THE STORY TO BE ABOUT!
1. GOODY
2. BADDY
3. THEY FIGHT
4. GOODY WINS
WHEN YOU'RE MAKING UP A HERO, THINK ABOUT WHAT THEY WANT -
WHAT IS THEIR GOAL?
TO FIGHT CRIME!
TO SOLVE MYSTERIES!
CAKE!
BUT YOU SHOULD ALSO THINK ABOUT WHY - WHAT MAKES THEM DO WHAT THEY DO?
SNIFF - WHEN I WAS A LITTLE BOY, SOMEONE STOLE MY TEDDY BEAR.
SO I GREW UP AND SWORE TO MAKE ALL CRIMINALS PAY.
ASKING QUESTIONS ABOUT YOUR CHARACTER HELPS YOU TO FIGURE OUT WHO THEY ARE.
AND ALSO IS FUN!
FOR INSTANCE! LET'S FIRE UP THE OL' AWESOME-O-TRON, AND CREATE...
NOW, BY ASKING QUESTIONS...
...YOU START TO FLESH OUT YOUR CHARACTER!
AND THOSE QUESTIONS THROW UP MORE QUESTIONS:
...ALL OF WHICH CAN GIVE YOU IDEAS FOR COOL STORIES!
NINJA MERMAID
Q: WHERE DOES SHE LIVE?
IN A COOL UNDERWATER PAGODA!
Q: WHAT IF IT GOT INVADED?
BY KUNG FU SHARKS?
Q: WHO IS HER FAMILY?
THE (NINJA) KING AND QUEEN OF ATLANTIS!
Q: WHAT IF THEY WERE KIDNAPPED?
BY SOMEONE WHO WANTED TO STEAL THE THRONE!
Q: WHO ARE HER FRIENDS?
A SUBMARINE EXPLORER AND HIS PET ROBOT JELLYFISH!
Q: HOW DID THEY MEET?
MAYBE SHE SAVED THEM?
LIKE FROM A KRAKEN!
STORIES!
AND THAT'S JUST THE START!
THE MORE QUESTIONS YOU ASK, THE BETTER!
WHAT DO THEY LIKE?
WHAT DO THEY HATE?
DO THEY HAVE ANY PETS?
WHAT'S THEIR FAVORITE BREAKFAST?
OOK!*
* ALL RIGHT THAT'S ENOUGH! I HAVE TO DRAW ALL THESE.

ART MONKEY CHALLENGE!

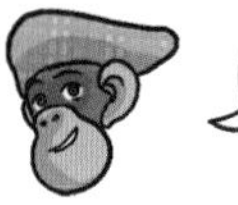
OOK!*

*OKAY, GUYS – IT'S YOUR TURN!

HERE'S A WEIRD-LOOKING CHARACTER I CREATED EARLIER – ANSWER THE QUESTIONS IN THE BOXES AND THEN TRY COMING UP WITH SOME STORIES USING YOUR ANSWERS!

WHAT IS HIS ***NAME?***

DOES HE HAVE ANY ***PETS?***

WHERE IS HE ***FROM?***

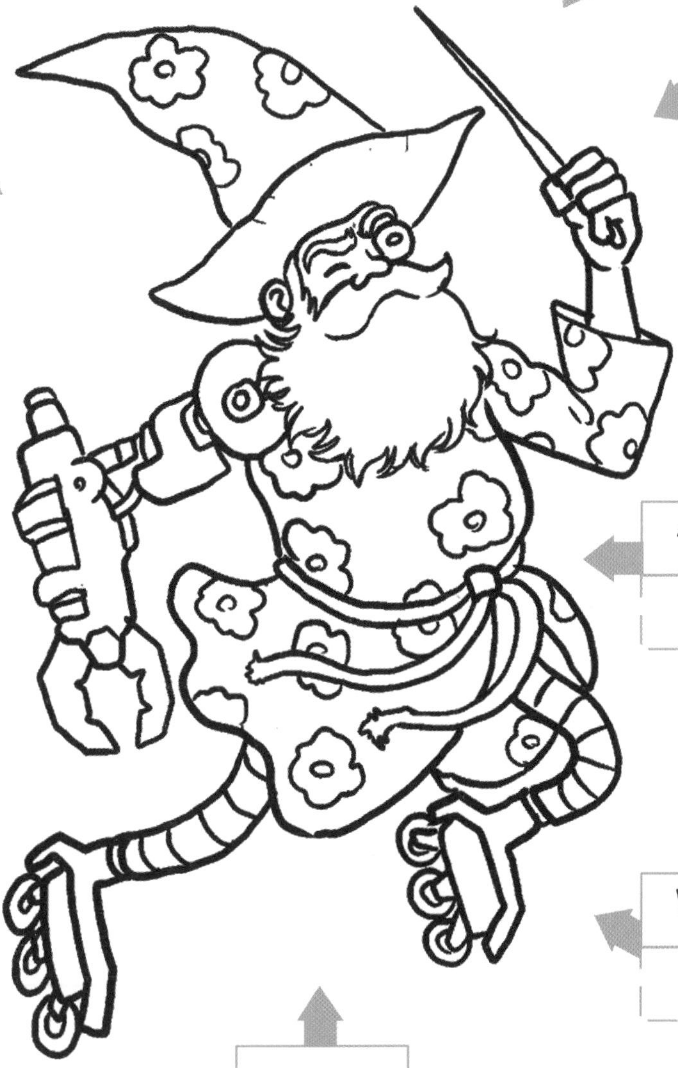

WHO'S HIS ***BEST FRIEND?***

ANY ***SPECIAL SKILLS?***

DOES HE HAVE A FAMILY?

WHAT DOES HE LIKE ON HIS ***PIZZA?***

WHAT IS HIS ***GREATEST FEAR?***

ANY SECRET ***WEAKNESSES?***

WHAT'S THE DEAL WITH THOSE ***WEIRD LEGS?***

18: HOW TO CREATE (AWESOME) VILLAINS

SO NOW YOU KNOW ALL ABOUT HOW TO CREATE YOUR OWN AWESOME HEROES!

BUT WHAT DOES EVERY GOOD HERO NEED?

1. GOODY 2. BADDY 3. THEY FIGHT 4. GOODY WINS

A *VILLAIN!* SOMEONE TO PLAGUE, PESTER, AND CREATE PROBLEMS FOR THEM!

THE MADDER, CRAZIER, AND CREEPIER THE BETTER!

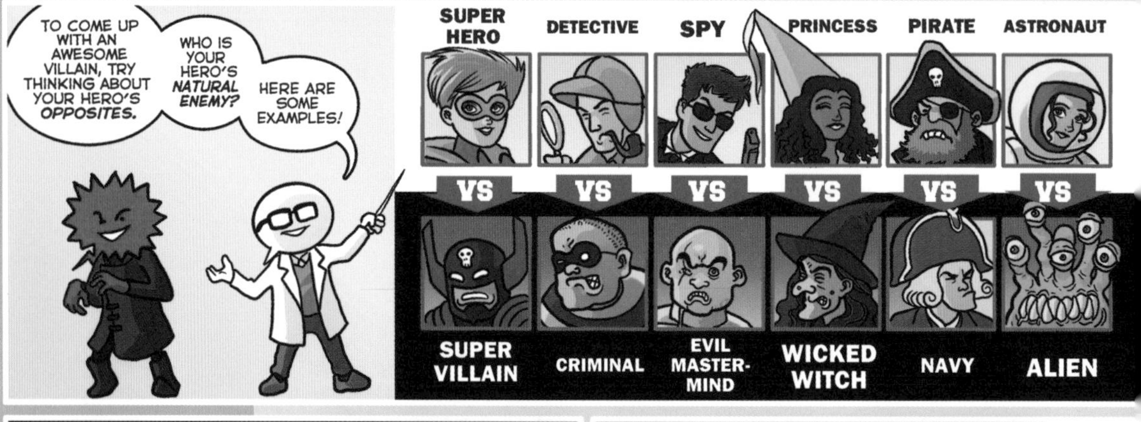

TO COME UP WITH AN AWESOME VILLAIN, TRY THINKING ABOUT YOUR HERO'S OPPOSITES.

WHO IS YOUR HERO'S *NATURAL ENEMY?*

HERE ARE SOME EXAMPLES!

SUPER HERO	DETECTIVE	SPY	PRINCESS	PIRATE	ASTRONAUT
VS	VS	VS	VS	VS	VS
SUPER VILLAIN	CRIMINAL	EVIL MASTER-MIND	WICKED WITCH	NAVY	ALIEN

WHEN DESIGNING A VILLAIN, USE THINGS THAT ARE CREEPY, WEIRD, OR SCARY!

STUFF LIKE THIS!

GIANT BRAINS · SLIME · SPIDERS · SPIKES · BANK ROBBERS · SKULLS · FIRE · VAMPIRES · MAD PROFESSORS · ZOMBIES · MONSTERS · MUMMIES · CREEPY CRAWLIES · CLOWNS · WEREWOLVES

STUFF THAT IS SCARY!

...BUT MAYBE DON'T USE *ALL* OF THEM AT ONCE!

OOK!

ART MONKEY CHALLENGE!

OOK!*

* HERE IS A BRAND-NEW HERO: THE INCREDIBLE...

SPACE VET

VS

USE THE PROF'S TIPS TO MAKE UP AN AWESOME NEW VILLAIN TO CAUSE PROBLEMS FOR HER!

APPENDIX ALERT

TURN TO PAGE 60

NEED SOME INSPIRATION? FOR SOME CREEPY VILLAIN IDEAS CHECK OUT APPENDIX E!

LESSON 19: CREATING (AWESOME) DRAMA

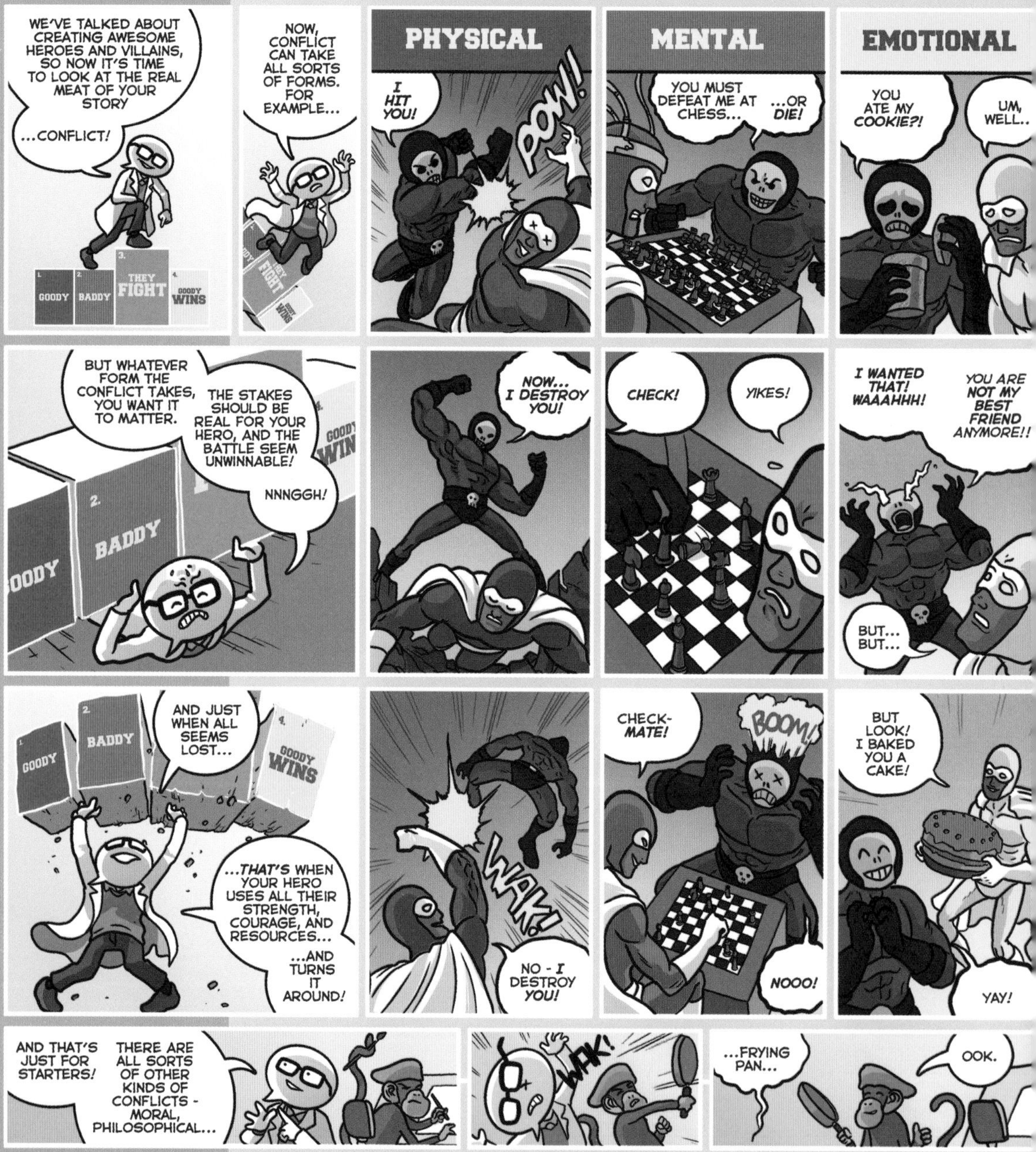

WE'VE TALKED ABOUT CREATING AWESOME HEROES AND VILLAINS, SO NOW IT'S TIME TO LOOK AT THE REAL MEAT OF YOUR STORY
...CONFLICT!
1. GOODY
2. BADDY
3. THEY FIGHT
4. GOODY WINS
NOW, CONFLICT CAN TAKE ALL SORTS OF FORMS. FOR EXAMPLE...
PHYSICAL
I HIT YOU!
POW!
MENTAL
YOU MUST DEFEAT ME AT CHESS...
...OR DIE!
EMOTIONAL
YOU ATE MY COOKIE?!
UM, WELL...
BUT WHATEVER FORM THE CONFLICT TAKES, YOU WANT IT TO MATTER.
THE STAKES SHOULD BE REAL FOR YOUR HERO, AND THE BATTLE SEEM UNWINNABLE!
NNNGGH!
NOW... I DESTROY YOU!
CHECK!
YIKES!
I WANTED THAT! WAAAHHH!
YOU ARE NOT MY BEST FRIEND ANYMORE!!
BUT... BUT...
AND JUST WHEN ALL SEEMS LOST...
...THAT'S WHEN YOUR HERO USES ALL THEIR STRENGTH, COURAGE, AND RESOURCES...
...AND TURNS IT AROUND!
WAK!
NO - I DESTROY YOU!
CHECK-MATE!
BOOM!
NOOO!
BUT LOOK! I BAKED YOU A CAKE!
YAY!
AND THAT'S JUST FOR STARTERS!
THERE ARE ALL SORTS OF OTHER KINDS OF CONFLICTS - MORAL, PHILOSOPHICAL...
WAK!
...FRYING PAN...
OOK.

ART MONKEY CHALLENGE!

 *OOK!**

* HERE ARE TWO CHARACTERS WHO LOOK LIKE THEY'RE NOT GOING TO GET ALONG. NOW IT'S UP TO YOU TO PUT THEM INTO CONFLICT!

TRY DRAWING YOUR OWN COMIC ABOUT WHAT HAPPENS WHEN THESE GUYS MEET!

USE THE QUESTIONS AT THE BOTTOM TO HELP YOU FIGURE OUT YOUR STORY IF YOU'RE STUCK!

 **VS** **ROBO BEAR**

HOW DO THEY MEET?

WHAT ARE THEY FIGHTING OVER?

WHERE IS THIS HAPPENING?

WHAT FORM DOES THEIR CONFLICT TAKE?

WHO WINS?

CHAIN SAW FIGHT?

ARGUMENT?

VIDEO GAME CONTEST?

LESSON 20: (AWESOME) ENDINGS

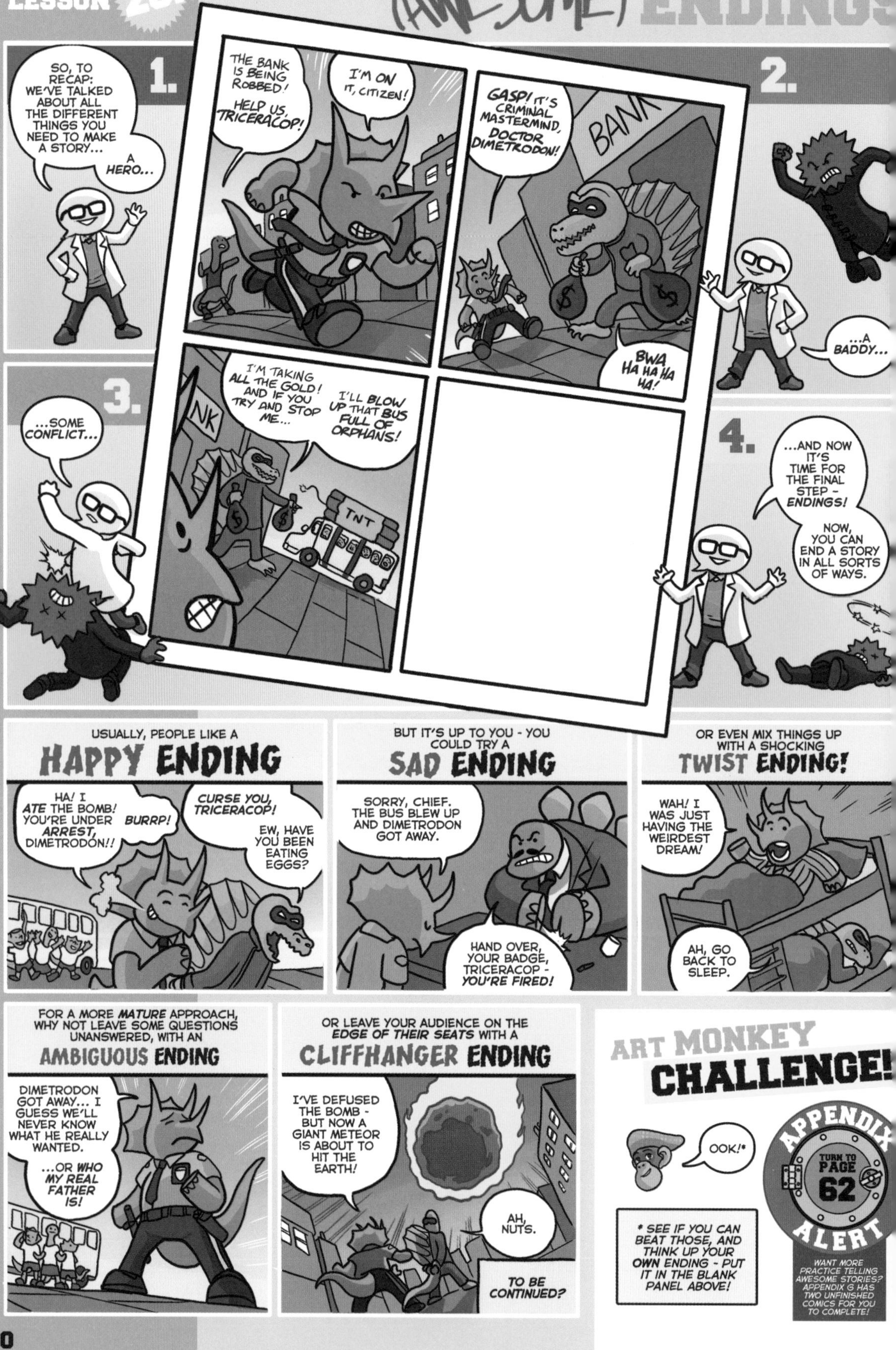
1.
SO, TO RECAP: WE'VE TALKED ABOUT ALL THE DIFFERENT THINGS YOU NEED TO MAKE A STORY...
A HERO...
THE BANK IS BEING ROBBED! HELP US, TRICERACOP!
I'M ON IT, CITIZEN!
2.
GASP! IT'S CRIMINAL MASTERMIND, DOCTOR DIMETRODON!
BANK
BWA HA HA HA HA!
...A BADDY...
3.
...SOME CONFLICT...
NK
I'M TAKING ALL THE GOLD! AND IF YOU TRY AND STOP ME...
I'LL BLOW UP THAT BUS FULL OF ORPHANS!
TNT
4.
...AND NOW IT'S TIME FOR THE FINAL STEP - ENDINGS!
NOW, YOU CAN END A STORY IN ALL SORTS OF WAYS.
USUALLY, PEOPLE LIKE A
HAPPY ENDING
HA! I ATE THE BOMB! YOU'RE UNDER ARREST, DIMETRODON!!
BURRP!
CURSE YOU, TRICERACOP!
EW, HAVE YOU BEEN EATING EGGS?
BUT IT'S UP TO YOU - YOU COULD TRY A
SAD ENDING
SORRY, CHIEF. THE BUS BLEW UP AND DIMETRODON GOT AWAY.
HAND OVER, YOUR BADGE, TRICERACOP - YOU'RE FIRED!
OR EVEN MIX THINGS UP WITH A SHOCKING
TWIST ENDING!
WAH! I WAS JUST HAVING THE WEIRDEST DREAM!
AH, GO BACK TO SLEEP.
FOR A MORE MATURE APPROACH, WHY NOT LEAVE SOME QUESTIONS UNANSWERED, WITH AN
AMBIGUOUS ENDING
DIMETRODON GOT AWAY... I GUESS WE'LL NEVER KNOW WHAT HE REALLY WANTED.
...OR WHO MY REAL FATHER IS!
OR LEAVE YOUR AUDIENCE ON THE EDGE OF THEIR SEATS WITH A
CLIFFHANGER ENDING
I'VE DEFUSED THE BOMB - BUT NOW A GIANT METEOR IS ABOUT TO HIT THE EARTH!
AH, NUTS.
TO BE CONTINUED?
ART MONKEY CHALLENGE!
OOK!*
* SEE IF YOU CAN BEAT THOSE, AND THINK UP YOUR OWN ENDING - PUT IT IN THE BLANK PANEL ABOVE!
APPENDIX ALERT
TURN TO PAGE 62
WANT MORE PRACTICE TELLING AWESOME STORIES? APPENDIX G HAS TWO UNFINISHED COMICS FOR YOU TO COMPLETE!

YOU'RE ALMOST THERE! YOU'VE GOT ALL THE KNOW-HOW YOU NEED TO WRITE AND DRAW YOUR OWN COMICS. YOU JUST NEED TO PUT IT ALL TOGETHER, WITH...

CHAPTER 6

HOW TO MAKE

YOUR VERY OWN COMICS

(...WHICH ARE AWESOME)

21: HOW TO MAKE YOUR VERY OWN COMICS

(...WHICH ARE AWESOME)

WE'VE LOOKED AT ALL THE DIFFERENT ASPECTS OF MAKING COMICS IN THESE LESSONS...

HOW TO HAVE IDEAS AND MAKE UP **CHARACTERS**...

THING THAT IS AWESOME + THING THAT IS AWESOME

THING THAT IS = TOTALLY SUPER AWESOME

HOW TO TURN THOSE IDEAS INTO **STORIES**...

1.	2.
GOODY	BADDY
3.	4.
THEY FIGHT	GOODY WINS

...AND, OF COURSE, HOW TO ACTUALLY **DRAW STUFF!**

...AND NOW IT'S TIME TO PUT IT ALL TOGETHER, AND LEARN HOW TO MAKE YOUR **VERY OWN COMIC!**

---

1 THE **TECHNICAL** BIT!

TAKE A PIECE OF PAPER.

FOLD IT IN HALF.

TA-DA! YOU NOW HAVE A BLANK FOUR-PAGE COMIC, JUST WAITING TO BE DRAWN IN!

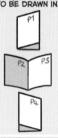
P1 · P2 · P3 · P4

AND IF YOU ADD A SECOND SHEET OF PAPER, YOU CAN MAKE AN EIGHT-PAGE COMIC!

P7 · P5 · P1 · P3

3 SHEETS = **12** PAGES

4 SHEETS = **16** PAGES

...AND SO ON. FOR EXAMPLE, AN ISSUE OF THE AWESOME PHOENIX COMIC HAS 32 PAGES – 8 SHEETS!

HOWEVER MANY SHEETS YOU USE, JUST REMEMBER: THE ONE ON THE OUTSIDE WILL BE THE FRONT AND BACK COVERS...

...AND THE ONE IN THE MIDDLE WILL BE THE CENTER SPREAD – THAT'S A GOOD PLACE FOR POSTERS AND STUFF...

---

2 THE **CREATIVE** BIT!

SO FIRST, THINK OF A **NAME** FOR YOUR COMIC...

THE DRAGON · THE ZAP! · THE BUMBO · THE MONKEY

...AND DRAW A **LOGO!**

NOW DECIDE WHAT TO PUT IN IT!

SHORT, FUNNY STRIPS?

LONGER, ADVENTURE STORIES?

OR A MIX OF BOTH?

AND WHAT **KIND** OF STORIES?

Sci-fi? · COMEDY? · Soap Opera? · FANTASY?

OR MAYBE EVEN SOME **HISTORY** OR COOL **SCIENCE?**

SERIOUS, SCARY, BONKERS – OR A BIT OF EVERYTHING?!

NEXT: WHO'S GOING TO **MAKE** IT?

ARE YOU GOING TO DO EVERY-THING YOURSELF?

OR WILL YOU BE THE EDITOR, AND GET ALL YOUR FRIENDS TO DRAW STORIES?

---

3 THE **NEXT** BIT!

HOORAY, YOU'VE MADE A COMIC! NOW WHAT DO YOU DO WITH IT?

YOU COULD USE A PHOTOCOPIER OR PRINTER TO MAKE COPIES OF IT!

THEN YOU CAN GIVE COPIES TO YOUR FRIENDS! YOU COULD EVEN **SELL** THEM! YOU'LL BE **RICH!***

*NOTE: YOU MIGHT NOT GET RICH. NOT **IMMEDIATELY**, ANYWAY.

YOU COULD EVEN PUT YOUR COMICS ON THE **INTERNET!**

JUST THINK, THEN PEOPLE ALL OVER THE WORLD WOULD BE ABLE TO READ **YOUR** COMICS!

THERE'S NOTHING STOPPING YOU! GET GOING!

CONQUER THE WORLD WITH COMICS!

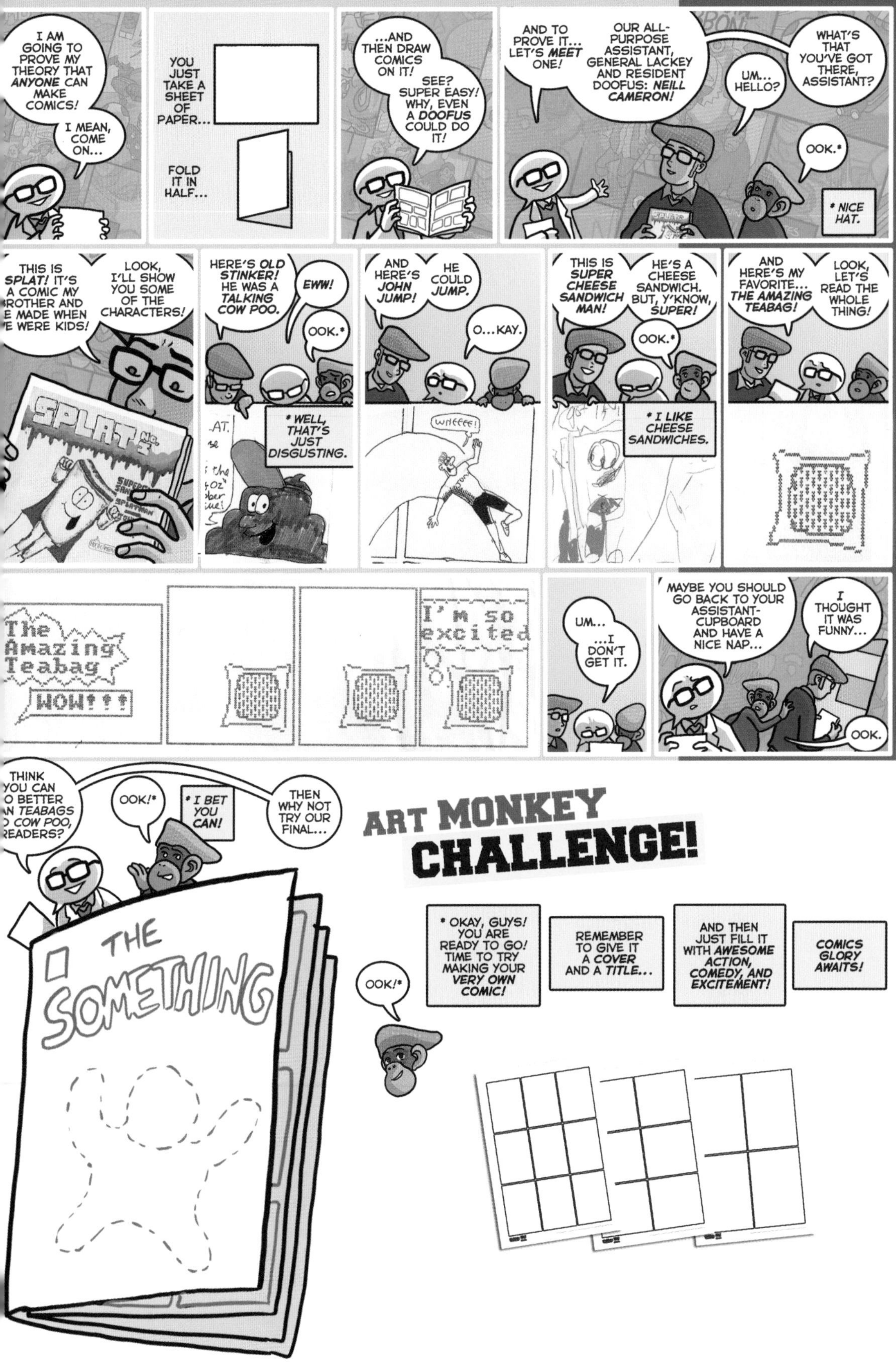

I AM GOING TO PROVE MY THEORY THAT ANYONE CAN MAKE COMICS!
I MEAN, COME ON...
YOU JUST TAKE A SHEET OF PAPER...
FOLD IT IN HALF...
...AND THEN DRAW COMICS ON IT!
SEE? SUPER EASY! WHY, EVEN A DOOFUS COULD DO IT!
AND TO PROVE IT... LET'S MEET ONE!
OUR ALL-PURPOSE ASSISTANT, GENERAL LACKEY AND RESIDENT DOOFUS: NEILL CAMERON!
UM... HELLO?
WHAT'S THAT YOU'VE GOT THERE, ASSISTANT?
OOK.*
* NICE HAT.
THIS IS SPLAT! IT'S A COMIC MY ROTHER AND E MADE WHEN E WERE KIDS!
LOOK, I'LL SHOW YOU SOME OF THE CHARACTERS!
SPLAT
HERE'S OLD STINKER! HE WAS A TALKING COW POO.
EWW!
OOK.*
* WELL, THAT'S JUST DISGUSTING.
AND HERE'S JOHN JUMP!
HE COULD JUMP.
O...KAY.
WHEEEE!
THIS IS SUPER CHEESE SANDWICH MAN!
HE'S A CHEESE SANDWICH. BUT, Y'KNOW, SUPER!
OOK.*
* I LIKE CHEESE SANDWICHES.
AND HERE'S MY FAVORITE... THE AMAZING TEABAG!
LOOK, LET'S READ THE WHOLE THING!
The Amazing Teabag
WOW!!!
I'm so excited
UM... ...I DON'T GET IT.
MAYBE YOU SHOULD GO BACK TO YOUR ASSISTANT-CUPBOARD AND HAVE A NICE NAP...
I THOUGHT IT WAS FUNNY...
OOK.
THINK YOU CAN O BETTER AN TEABAGS D COW POO, READERS?
OOK!*
* I BET YOU CAN!
THEN WHY NOT TRY OUR FINAL...
ART MONKEY CHALLENGE!
THE SOMETHING
OOK!*
* OKAY, GUYS! YOU ARE READY TO GO! TIME TO TRY MAKING YOUR VERY OWN COMIC!
REMEMBER TO GIVE IT A COVER AND A TITLE...
AND THEN JUST FILL IT WITH AWESOME ACTION, COMEDY, AND EXCITEMENT!
COMICS GLORY AWAITS!

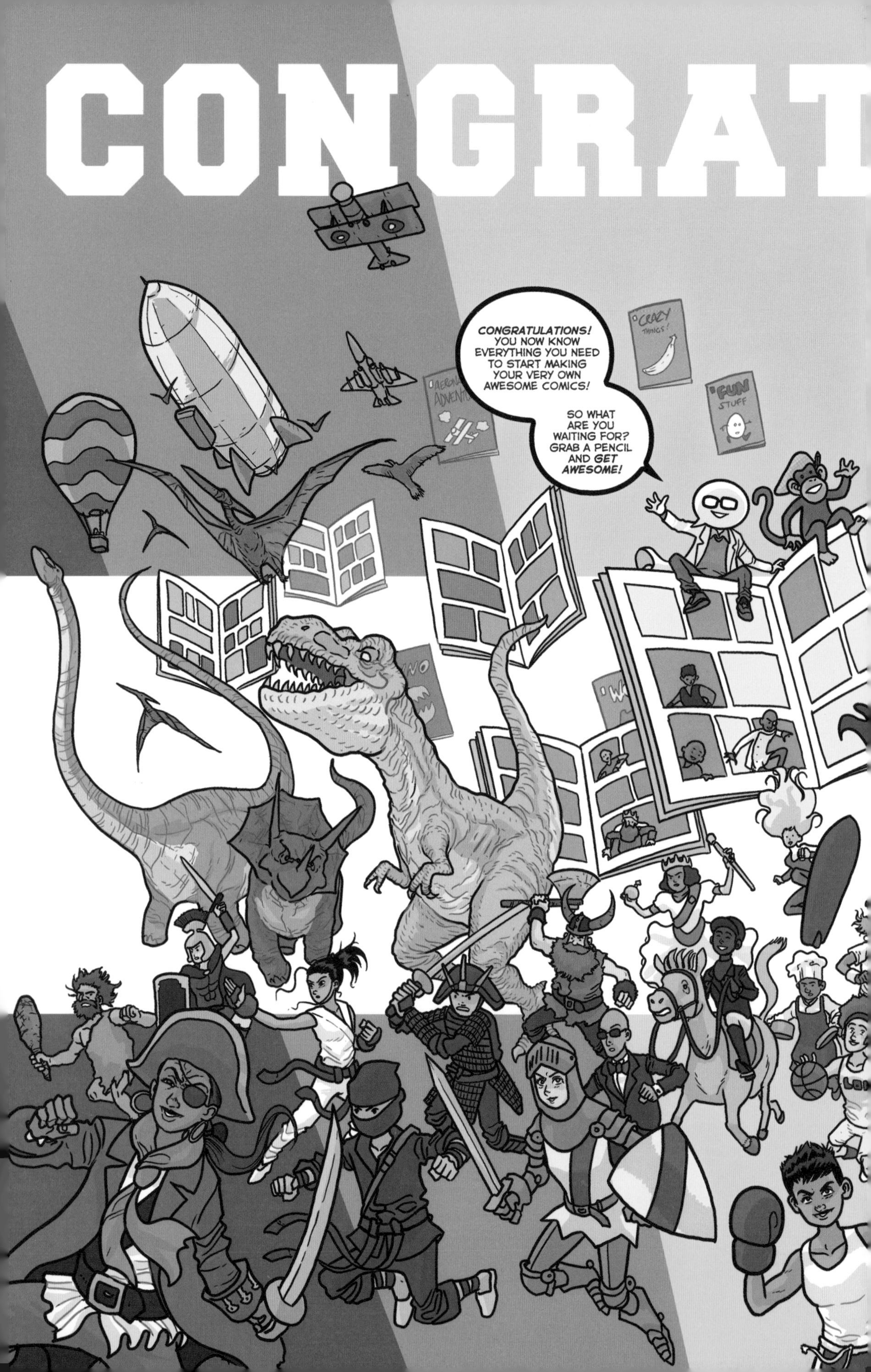
CONGRAT
CONGRATULATIONS! YOU NOW KNOW EVERYTHING YOU NEED TO START MAKING YOUR VERY OWN AWESOME COMICS!
SO WHAT ARE YOU WAITING FOR? GRAB A PENCIL AND GET AWESOME!
CRAZY THINGS!
FUN STUFF

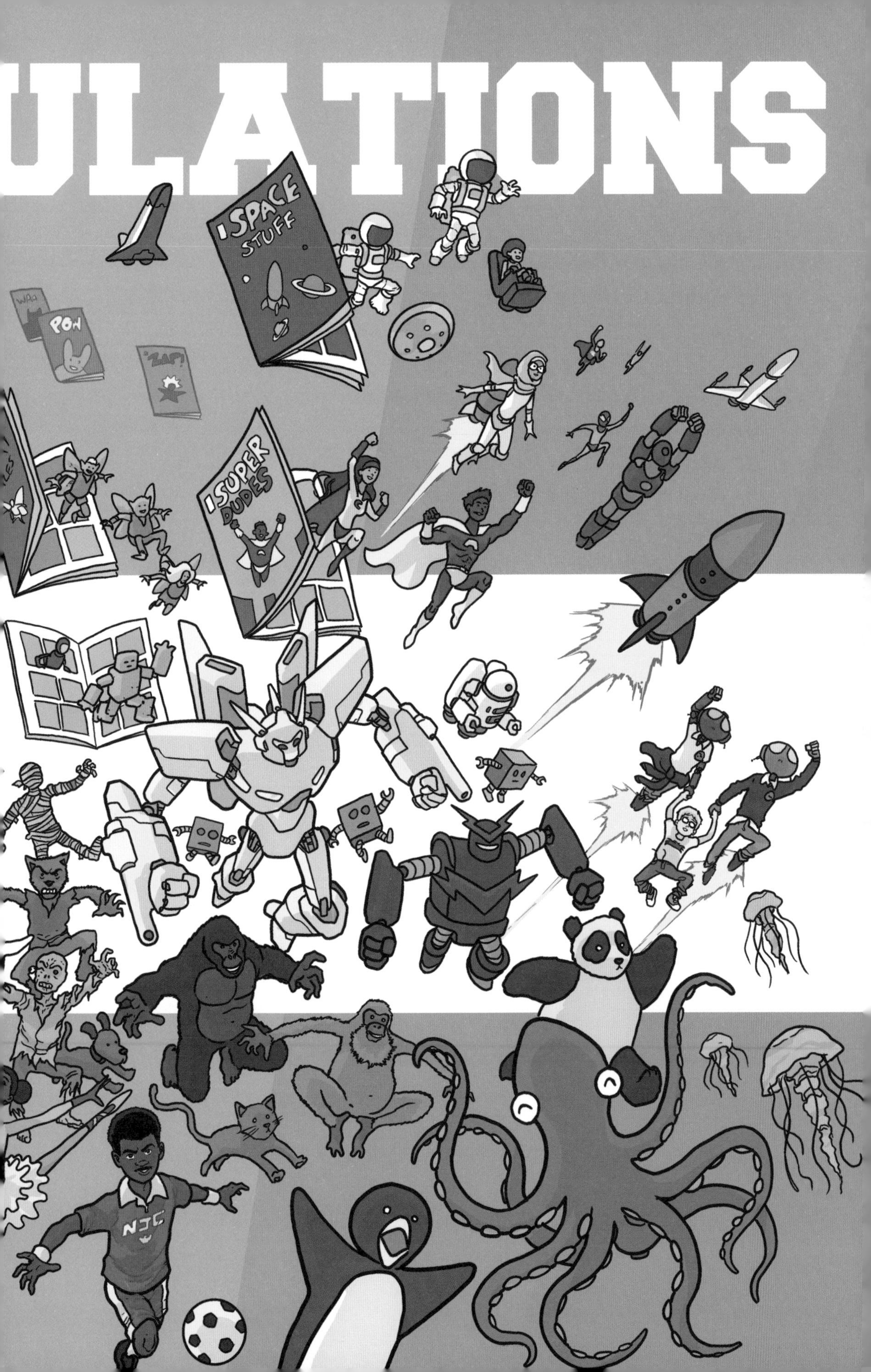
ULATIONS
SPACE STUFF
POW
ZAP!
SUPER DUDES
NJC

MORE (AWESOME) STUFF

APPENDIX A MORE STUFF THAT IS AWESOME

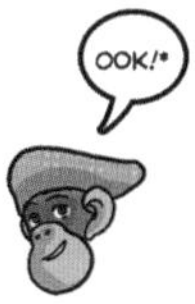
OOK!*

*TRY MIXING AND MATCHING SOME OF THESE INGREDIENTS TO CREATE AWESOME NEW CHARACTERS!

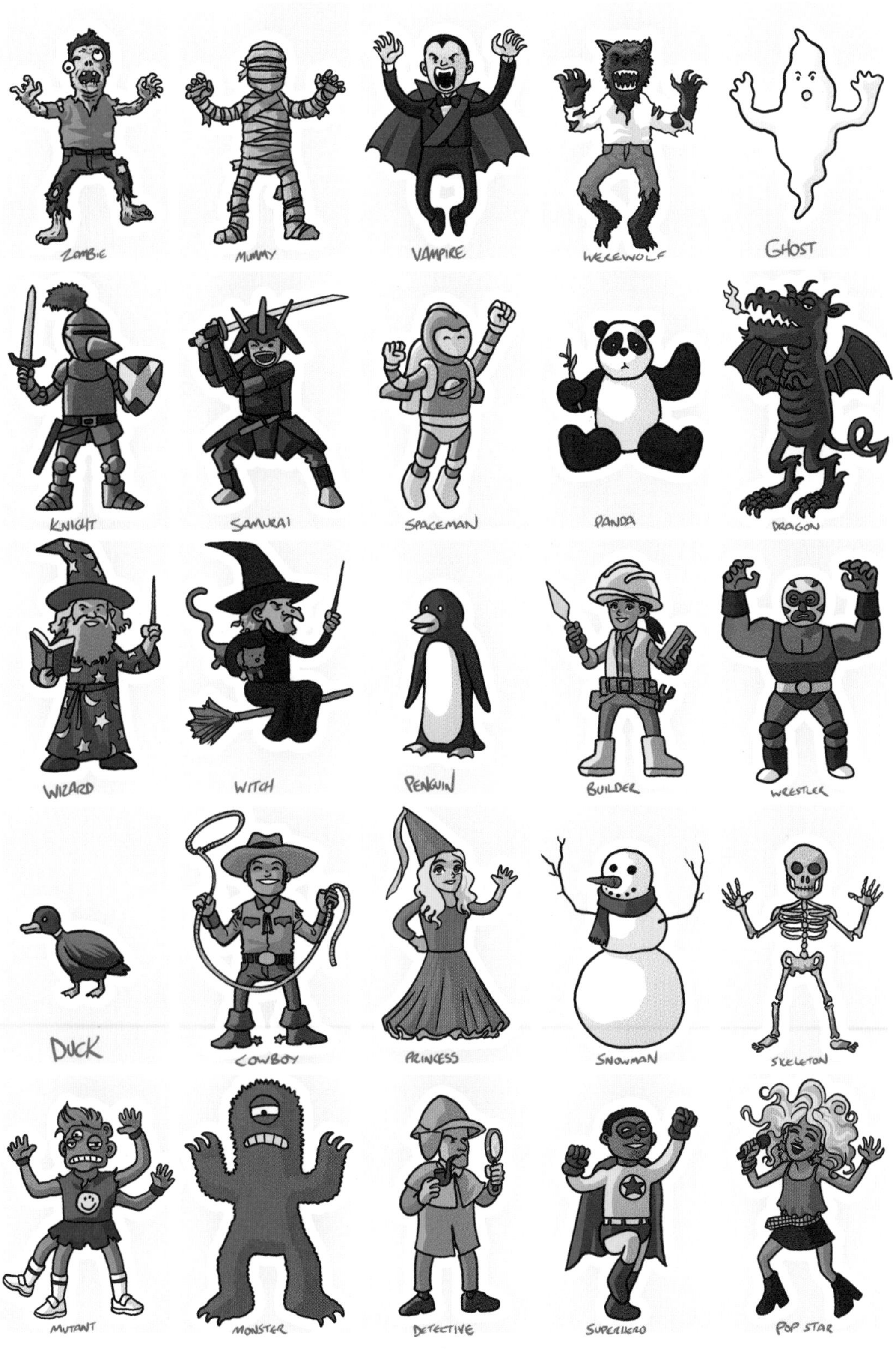
ZOMBIE
MUMMY
VAMPIRE
WEREWOLF
GHOST
KNIGHT
SAMURAI
SPACEMAN
PANDA
DRAGON
WIZARD
WITCH
PENGUIN
BUILDER
WRESTLER
DUCK
COWBOY
PRINCESS
SNOWMAN
SKELETON
MUTANT
MONSTER
DETECTIVE
SUPERHERO
POP STAR

APPENDIX B

INVENTORY OF COOL ROBOT ACCESSORIES

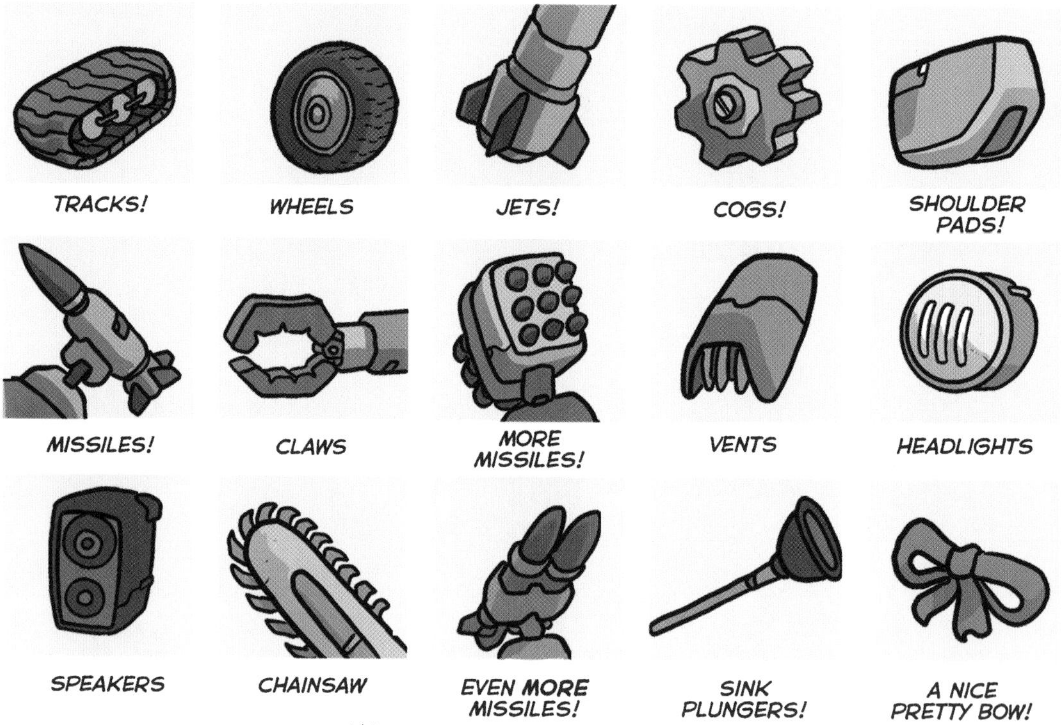
TRACKS!
WHEELS
JETS!
COGS!
SHOULDER PADS!
MISSILES!
CLAWS
MORE MISSILES!
VENTS
HEADLIGHTS
SPEAKERS
CHAINSAW
EVEN MORE MISSILES!
SINK PLUNGERS!
A NICE PRETTY BOW!

APPENDIX C

INVENTORY OF PIRATE MUSTACHERY

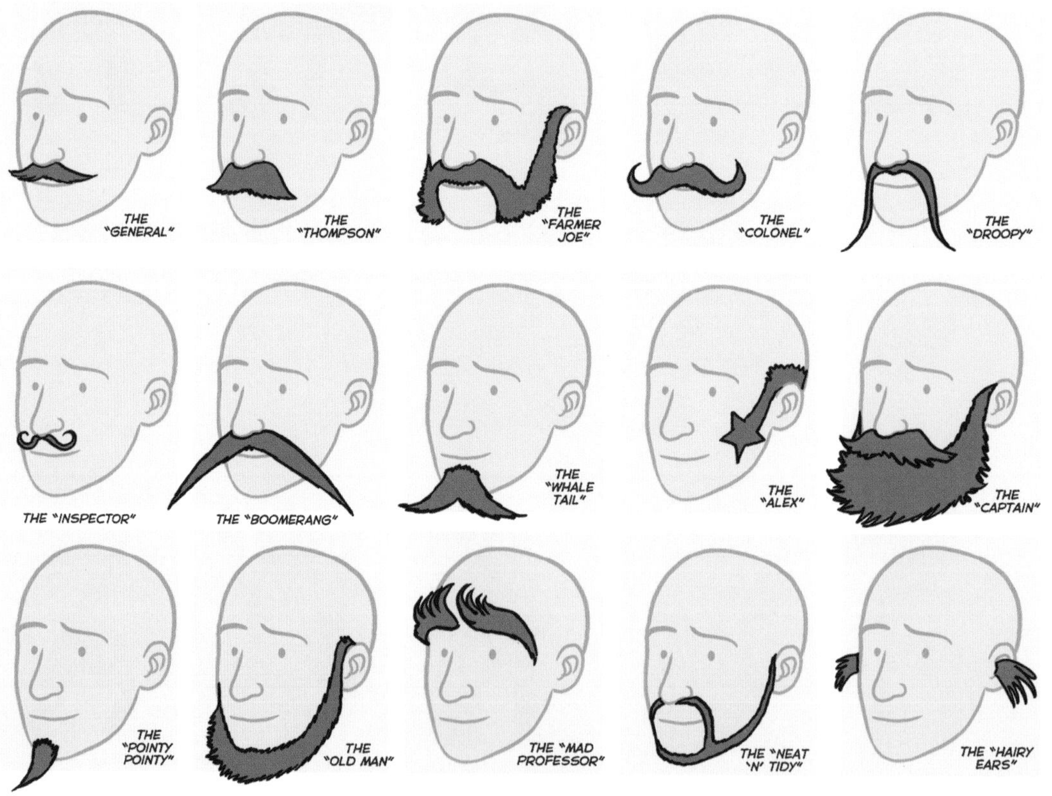
THE "GENERAL"
THE "THOMPSON"
THE "FARMER JOE"
THE "COLONEL"
THE "DROOPY"
THE "INSPECTOR"
THE "BOOMERANG"
THE "WHALE TAIL"
THE "ALEX"
THE "CAPTAIN"
THE "POINTY POINTY"
THE "OLD MAN"
THE "MAD PROFESSOR"
THE "NEAT 'N' TIDY"
THE "HAIRY EARS"

APPENDIX D HOW TO DRAW

DINOSAURS

STEP-BY-STEP

DIPLODOCUS

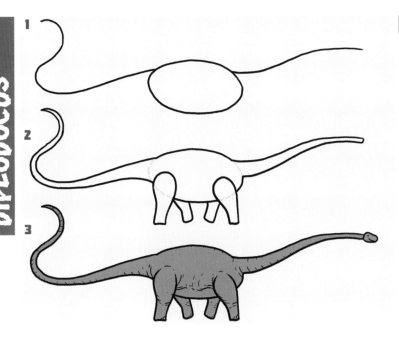

1

2

3

APATOSAURUS

(SAME BASIC SHAPE, BUT SQUATTER, BULKIER)

BRACHIOSAURUS

(TALLER, MORE UPRIGHT)

1

2

3

4

5

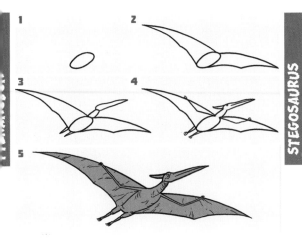

STEGOSAURUS

1

2

3

4

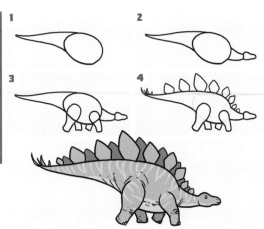

APPENDIX E STEP-BY-STEP CREEPY CREATURES

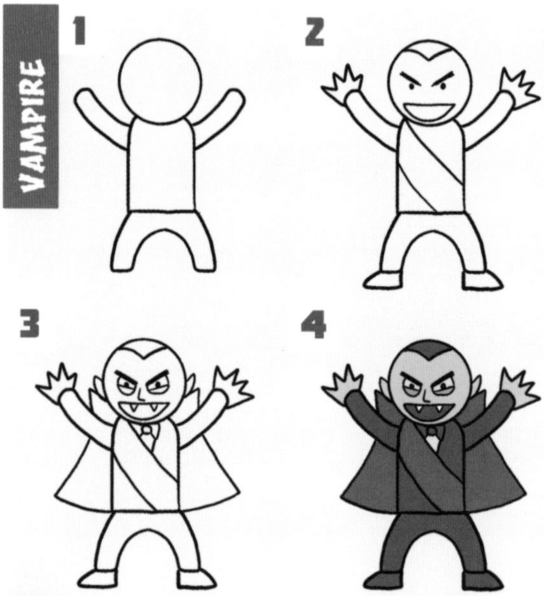
VAMPIRE
1
2
3
4

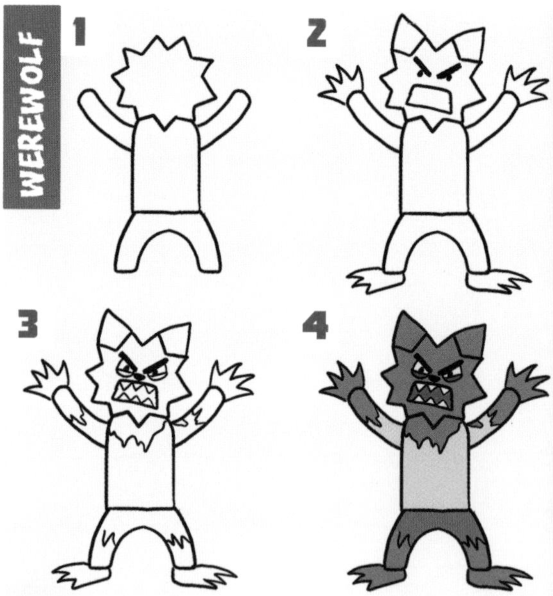
WEREWOLF
1
2
3
4

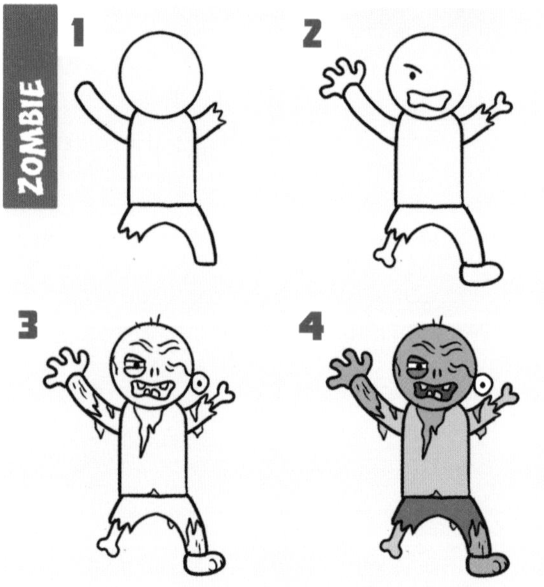
ZOMBIE
1
2
3
4

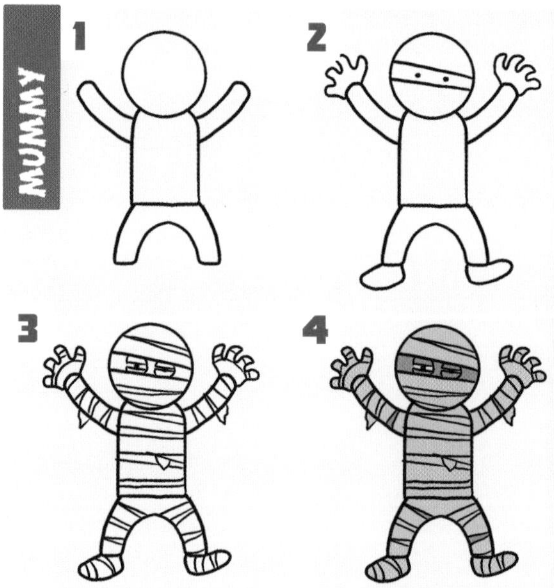
MUMMY
1
2
3
4

APPENDIX  STEP-BY-STEP
PENGUINS

1

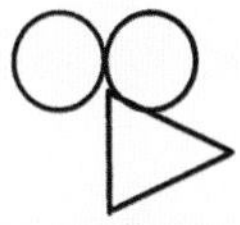

2

3

4

5

6

AWESOME PENGUIN VARIANTS

NINJA

CHEF

SAILOR

APPENDIX G

MORE FUN COMICS!

EXTRA ART MONKEY CHALLENGE

OOK!*

* HERE ARE A COUPLE MORE COMIC STRIPS FOR YOU TO FINISH OFF!

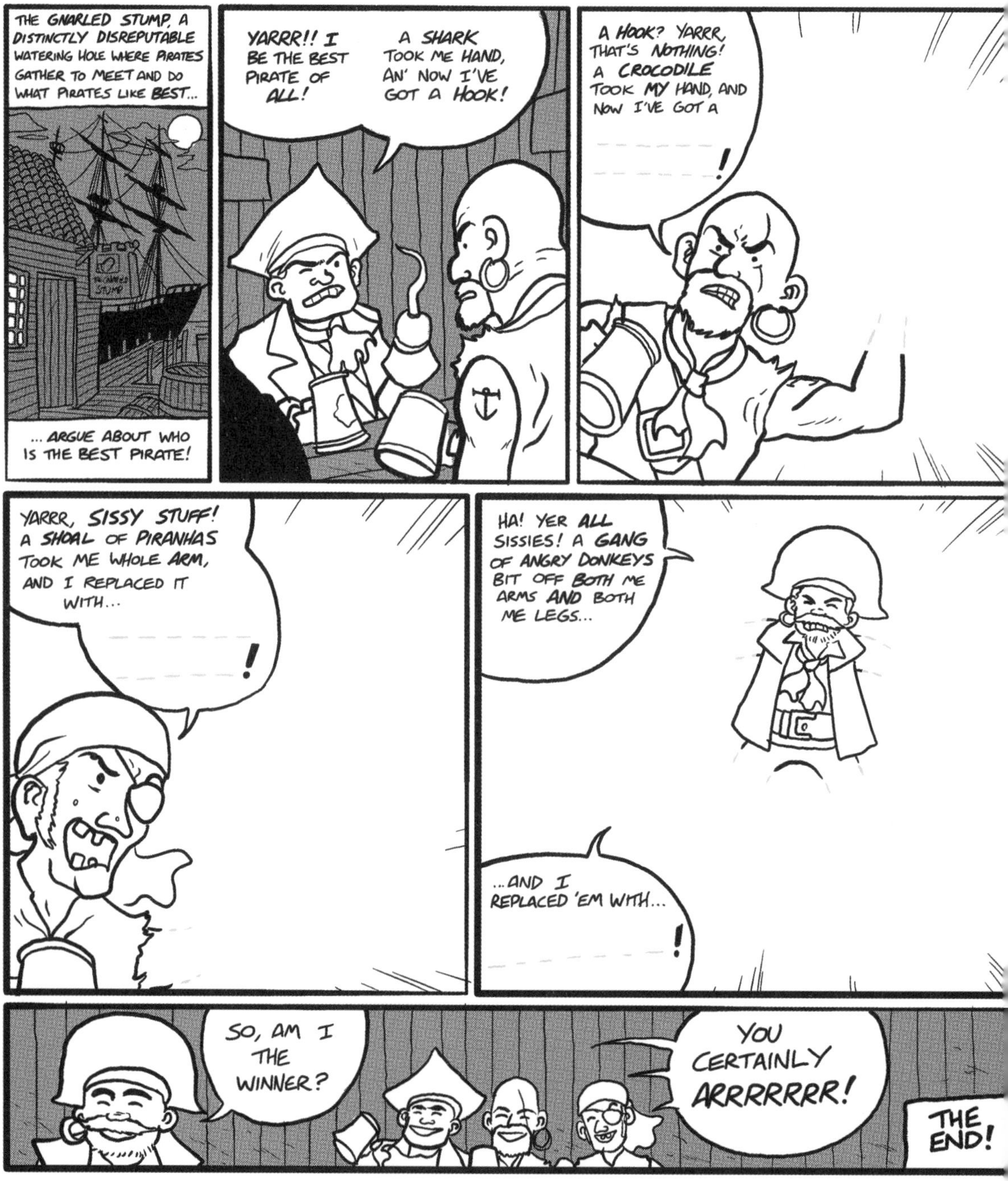

THE GNARLED STUMP, A DISTINCTLY DISREPUTABLE WATERING HOLE WHERE PIRATES GATHER TO MEET AND DO WHAT PIRATES LIKE BEST...
... ARGUE ABOUT WHO IS THE BEST PIRATE!
YARRR!! I BE THE BEST PIRATE OF ALL!
A SHARK TOOK ME HAND, AN' NOW I'VE GOT A HOOK!
A HOOK? YARRR, THAT'S NOTHING! A CROCODILE TOOK MY HAND, AND NOW I'VE GOT A ________ !
YARRR, SISSY STUFF! A SHOAL OF PIRANHAS TOOK ME WHOLE ARM, AND I REPLACED IT WITH... ________ !
HA! YER ALL SISSIES! A GANG OF ANGRY DONKEYS BIT OFF BOTH ME ARMS AND BOTH ME LEGS...
...AND I REPLACED 'EM WITH... ________ !
SO, AM I THE WINNER?
YOU CERTAINLY ARRRRRRR!
THE END!

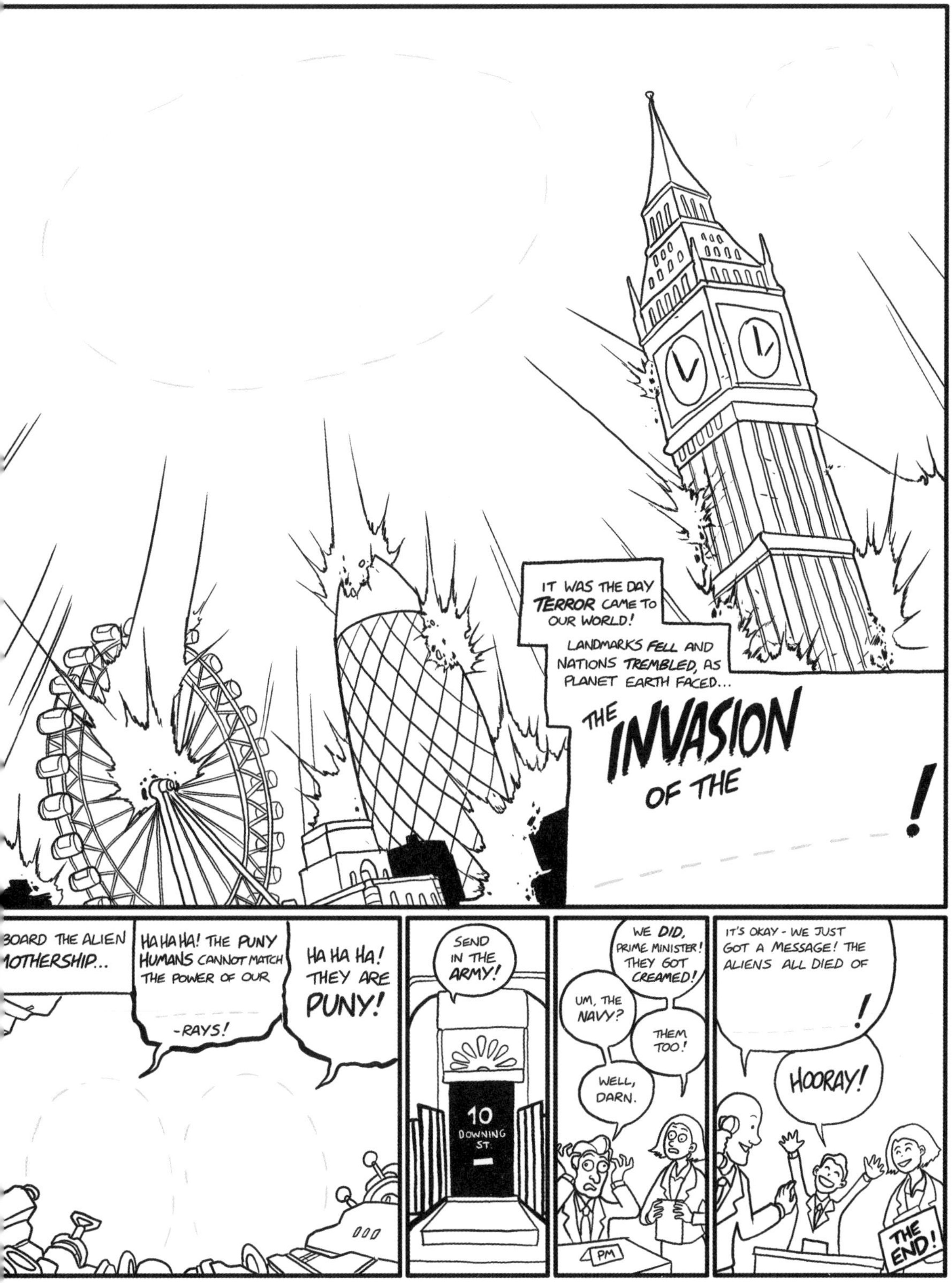
IT WAS THE DAY TERROR CAME TO OUR WORLD!
LANDMARKS FELL AND NATIONS TREMBLED, AS PLANET EARTH FACED...
THE INVASION OF THE
!
BOARD THE ALIEN MOTHERSHIP...
HA HA HA! THE PUNY HUMANS CANNOT MATCH THE POWER OF OUR
-RAYS!
HA HA HA! THEY ARE PUNY!
SEND IN THE ARMY!
10 DOWNING ST.
UM, THE NAVY?
WE DID, PRIME MINISTER! THEY GOT CREAMED!
THEM TOO!
WELL, DARN.
PM
IT'S OKAY - WE JUST GOT A MESSAGE! THE ALIENS ALL DIED OF
!
HOORAY!
THE END!

APPENDIX H BONUS PINUP CHALLENGE

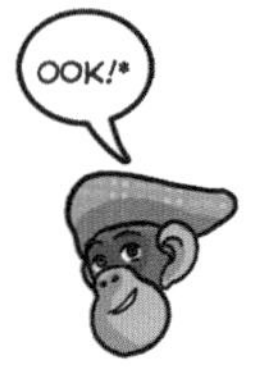
OOK!*

* **SOMETHING** IS CHASING PROF. P, ART MONKEY, AND THEIR PALS – BUT **WHAT?**

USE ALL YOUR **AWESOME ARTISTIC ABILITIES** TO FINISH THE DRAWING!

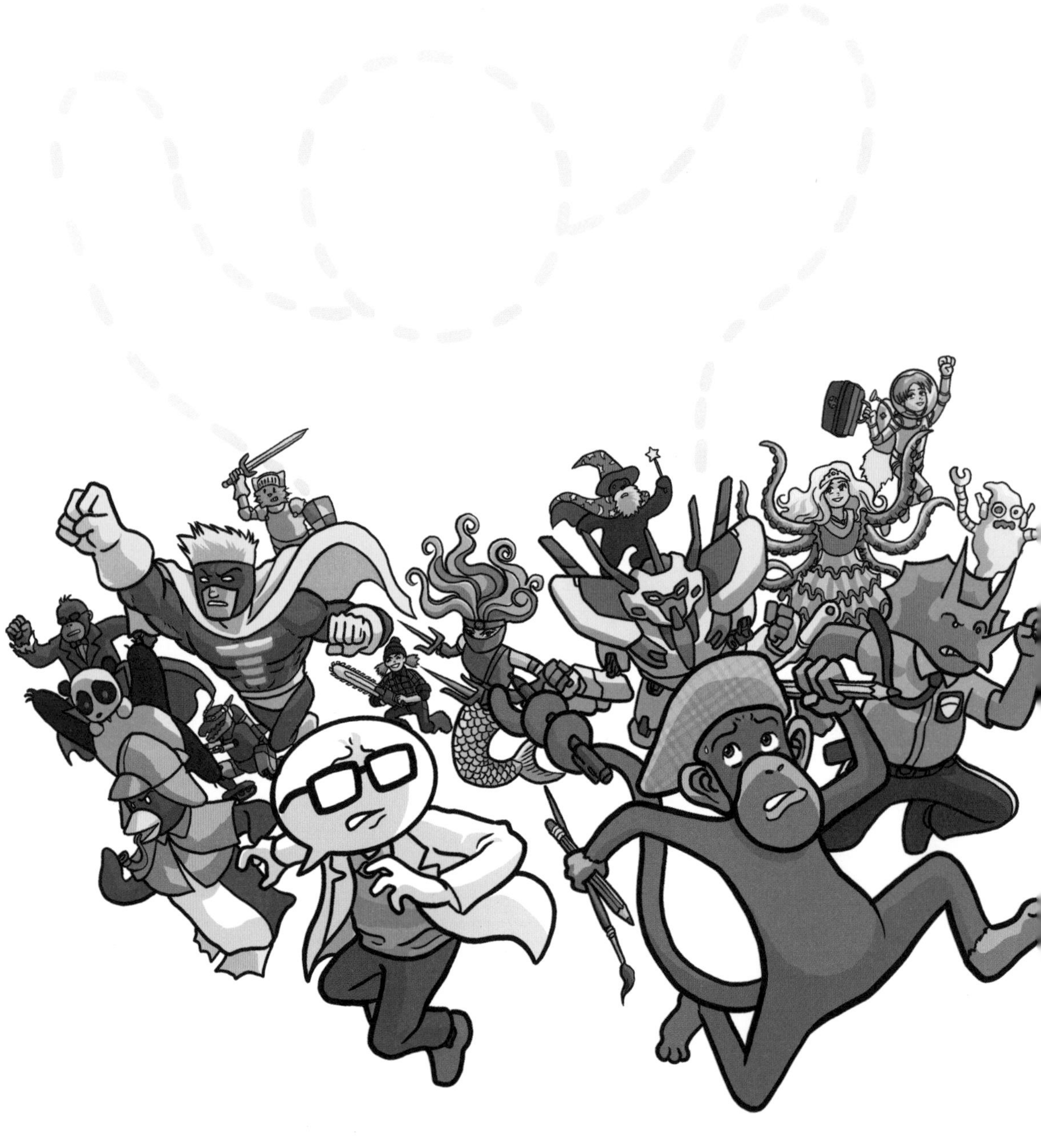